Eighth Edition

THE NEW JERSEY NOTARY LAW PRIMER

All the hard-to-find information every New Jersey Notary Public needs to know!

National Notary Association

Published by

National Notary Association
9350 De Soto Avenue
Chatsworth, CA 91311-4926
(800) 876-6827
Fax: (818) 700-0920
Website: www.NationalNotary.org
Email: nna@NationalNotary.org

©2015 National Notary Association
ALL RIGHTS RESERVED. No part of this book may be reproduced in any form without permission in writing from the publisher.

The information in this *Primer* is correct and current at the time of its publication, although new laws, regulations and rulings may subsequently affect the validity of certain sections. This information is provided to aid comprehension of state Notary Public requirements and should not be construed as legal advice. Please consult an attorney for inquiries relating to legal matters.

Eighth Edition ©2015
First Edition ©1994

ISBN: 978-1-59767-176-7

Table of Contents

Introduction 1

Notary Laws Explained 2

    The Notary Commission 2

    Official Notarial Acts 8

    Practices and Procedures...22

    Misconduct, Fines and Penalties 47

New Jersey Laws Pertaining to Notaries Public........................50

About the NNA 65

Index 67

Have a Tough Notary Question?

If you were a National Notary Association member, you could get the answer to that difficult question. Join the NNA® and your membership includes access to the NNA® Hotline* and live Notary experts providing the latest Notary information regarding laws, rules and regulations.

Hours
Monday – Friday   5:00 a.m.–7:00 p.m. (PT)
Saturday   5:00 a.m.–5:00 p.m. (PT)

NNA® Hotline Toll-Free Phone Number: 1-888-876-0827

After hours you can leave a message or email our experts at Hotline@NationalNotary.org and they will respond the next business day.

*Access to the NNA® Hotline is for National Notary Association members and NNA® Hotline subscribers only. Call and become a member today.

Introduction

You are to be commended on your interest in New Jersey Notary law! Purchasing *The New Jersey Notary Law Primer* identifies you as a conscientious professional who takes your official responsibilities seriously.

In few fields is the expression "more to it than meets the eye" truer than in Notary law. What often appears on the surface to be a simple procedure may, in fact, have important legal considerations.

The purpose of *The New Jersey Notary Law Primer* is to provide you with a resource to help decipher the many intricate laws that affect notarization. In doing so, the *Primer* will acquaint you with all important aspects of New Jersey's Notary law and with prudent Notary practices in general.

This edition of *The New Jersey Notary Law Primer* has been updated to include all pertinent law changes, including new restrictions and requirements regarding the unauthorized practice of law, effective December 2014, and new rules regarding electronic recording, effective November 2014.

The New Jersey Notary Law Primer takes you through the myriad of Notary laws and puts them in easy-to-understand terms. Every section of the law is analyzed and explained, as well as topics not covered by New Jersey law but nonetheless of vital concern to you as a Notary.

For handy reference, we have reprinted the complete text of the laws of New Jersey that relate to Notaries Public.

Whether you're about to be commissioned for the first time, or are a longtime Notary, we're sure *The New Jersey Notary Law Primer* will provide you with new insight and understanding. Your improved comprehension of New Jersey's Notary law will naturally result in your greater competence as a professional Notary Public.

Milton G. Valera
Chairman
National Notary Association

Notary Laws Explained

In layperson's language, this chapter discusses and clarifies key parts of the laws of New Jersey that regulate Notaries Public. Most of these laws are reprinted in full in "New Jersey Laws Pertaining to Notaries Public," beginning on page 50.

Additional information about New Jersey's requirements for Notaries Public is available on the Department of the Treasury's website. For step-by-step instructions on the commission application process, applicants also may visit *www.nationalnotary.org/new-jersey/become-a-notary*.

THE NOTARY COMMISSION

Application for New Commission

<u>Qualifications</u>. To become a Notary in New Jersey, whether as a first-time Notary or to renew a commission, the applicant (NJSA 52:7-12; 52:7-13):

- Must be at least 18 years old.

- Must be a resident of New Jersey, or be a resident of an adjoining state and maintain a place of business or office in New Jersey.

- Must not have been convicted in New Jersey or another state of an offense involving dishonesty or of a crime in the first or second degree.

<u>Endorsement</u>. The completed application form must be endorsed by a member of the New Jersey Legislature (NJSA 52:7-11).

Citizenship. U.S. citizenship is not required to become a New Jersey Notary, though any noncitizen applicant should be a permanent legal resident. A 1984 Supreme Court decision, *Bernal v. Fainter*, declared that no state may deny a Notary commission merely on the basis of lack of U.S. citizenship.

Denial of Application. No one may be appointed or reappointed as a New Jersey Notary who has been convicted of a crime of the second degree or above, of an offense involving dishonesty (e.g., forgery, counterfeiting) under the laws of New Jersey, or of a substantially similar crime under the laws of another state or of the United States (NJSA 52:7-20, 52:7-21).

Application Fee. A nonrefundable application fee of $25 must be submitted with the application. An additional fee will be required at the time of filing the Notary Public's certificate of commission and qualification with the county clerk (NJSA 22A:2-29).

Application Misstatement. As stated on the commission application, substantial and material misstatement or omission in the application for a Notary commission is reason for the State Treasurer to deny, revoke, or suspend a Notary's commission.

Qualification as a Delaware Notary. Residents of New Jersey who maintain or are regularly employed in an office in Delaware may qualify for a Delaware Notary commission. For more information, contact the Secretary of State at 401 Federal St., Suite 3, Dover, DE 19901, or by calling (302) 739-4111.

Qualification as a New York Notary. Residents of New Jersey who maintain or are regularly employed in an office in New York may qualify for a New York Notary commission. For more information, contact the Division of Licensing Services at 80 South Swan Street, Albany, NY 12210, or by calling (518) 474-4429.

Qualification as a Pennsylvania Notary. Residents of New Jersey who maintain or are regularly employed in an office in Pennsylvania may qualify for a Pennsylvania Notary commission. For more information, contact the Department of State, Bureau of Commissions, Elections and Legislation, Notary Division, at 210 North Office Building, Harrisburg, PA 17120, or by calling (717) 787-5280.

Application for Reappointment

Application. A Notary seeking reappointment must apply for a new commission and follow the same procedures as when applying for a commission for the first time (NJSA 52:7-11).

Usually — as long as the Notary's address information is correct in the state's records — the State Treasurer will automatically send the Notary a renewal package within three months of the current commission's expiration. However, the Notary is ultimately responsible for requesting a renewal package if the Notary wants to avoid a gap between commission terms.

Exam

Not Required. An exam is not required to obtain a new or renewed Notary commission. However, a Notary should study and be familiar with the laws of notarization in order to properly perform the duties expected of a Notary.

Notary Bond and Liability

Not Required. New Jersey Notaries are not required to obtain a surety bond.

Liability. As ministerial officials, Notaries generally may be held financially responsible for any and all damages caused by their mistakes or misconduct in performing notarial acts.

If a person is financially injured by a Notary's negligence or failure to properly execute a notarial act — whether performed intentionally or unintentionally — the Notary may be sued in civil court and ordered to pay all resulting damages, including attorneys' fees.

A person need not be named in a document in order to sue a Notary for damages resulting from the Notary's handling of that document. If, for example, a lender accepts a forged, notarized deed as collateral for a loan, the lender might sue to recover losses from the Notary who witnessed the notarized deed.

Penalties for Fraud. Willful violations involving fraud and dishonesty may lead to the revocation of a New Jersey Notary commission. The Notary will also be subject to civil and criminal actions (NJSA 2C:43-3).

Errors and Omissions Insurance. Notaries may choose to purchase insurance to cover any unintentional errors or omissions they may make. Notary errors and omissions insurance provides protection for Notaries who are involved in claims or sued for damages resulting from unintentional notarial errors and omissions. In the event of a claim or civil lawsuit, the insurance company will provide and pay for the Notary's legal counsel and absorb any damages levied by a court or agreed to in a settlement, up to the policy coverage limit. Generally, errors and omissions insurance does not cover the Notary for dishonest, fraudulent or criminal acts or omissions, or for willful or intentional disregard of the law.

Oath of Office

Requirement. New Jersey Notaries are required to take and file an oath of office before executing any acts as a Notary Public (NJSA 52:7-14).

Filing the Oath. The oath must be taken and filed with the clerk of the county in which the Notary resides within three months of the commission start date indicated on the Notary's certificate of commission and qualification. Nonresident applicants must take the oath before the clerk of the county in New Jersey in which the applicant maintains an office or is employed.

To take the oath, the applicant must bring the Notary's certificate of commission and qualification to the clerk of the county in which he or she resides or is employed. The clerk will then administer the required oath, in which the applicant swears to faithfully and honestly discharge the duties of the office of Notary Public for New Jersey.

Within 10 days after administering the oath, the county clerk returns the certificate of commission and qualification to the State Treasurer and records the "sworn date" in the county clerk's files (NJSA 52:7-14).

A Notary may choose to file additional copies of the certificate of commission and qualification in other counties. Although the Notary has statewide jurisdiction, filing additional certificates makes it easier for a county clerk to authenticate a Notary's commission if the Notary lives and works in different counties. However, filing duplicate certificates is not required (NJSA 52:7-15).

Fee. The county clerk will charge a fee to administer the oath and another fee to file and record it. The Notary applicant should contact the local county clerk to determine these fees (NJSA 22A:2-29).

Failure to File Oath of Office. A Notary Public must file his or her oath of office within three months after the date specified on the Notary Public's commission certificate. Failure to file within this time limit may result in cancellation or revocation of the appointment (NJSA 52:7-14).

Jurisdiction

Statewide. Resident and nonresident (living in an adjoining state and working in New Jersey) New Jersey Notaries may perform official acts throughout the state, but not beyond the state borders (NJSA 52:7-15).

A Notary may not witness a signing outside of New Jersey and then return to the state to perform the notarization. All parts of a given notarization must be performed at the same time and place within the state of New Jersey.

Term of Office

Five-Year Term. The term of office for a New Jersey Notary Public is five years. Each term begins on the date specified by the State Treasurer on the commission certificate and ends at midnight on its commission expiration date or as deemed necessary by the State Treasurer (NJSA 52:7-11).

Resignation

Notification. To resign, a Notary should submit a written notice to the State Treasurer, giving an effective date. Such a resignation is appropriate if the Notary moves and does not retain a place of business or office in New Jersey. It is recommended the notice be sent by certified mail.

The resignation notice may also be sent to the office of the clerk of the county where the Notary has filed the certificate of commission and qualification.

Disposition of Seal and Records. If the resigning Notary has a seal of office and/or a stamp that he or she used to affix information on Notary certificates, these should be destroyed or defaced to prevent fraudulent use. If the Notary maintained a journal of notarial acts or other recordbook, the State Treasurer recommends the Notary retain the journal or recordbook for a reasonable amount of time to reflect the statute of limitations.

Death of Notary

Notification. If a Notary dies, the Notary's personal representative should notify the State Treasurer. The notification should include the Notary's name and commission number, as well as any additional pertinent information, and should be sent by certified mail.

Disposition of Seal and Records. If the deceased Notary used a seal of office and/or a stamp to affix information on Notary certificates, these should be destroyed or defaced to prevent fraudulent use. If the Notary maintained a journal or other recordbook, the State Treasurer recommends that the Notary's personal representative retain the journal for a reasonable amount of time that reflects the statute of limitations.

Change of Address

Notification Required. When a Notary changes his or her address, notification must be made to the State Treasurer — and to all county clerks where copies of the certificate of commission and qualification are filed — before notarizing any documents.

Change of address forms are available at *www.state.nj.us/treasury/revenue/notarychange.pdf* or by calling (609) 292-9292.

The Notary must return the change of address form and a $25 fee (payable to the State Treasurer) by certified mail to:

> State of New Jersey
> Department of the Treasury
> Division of Revenue and Enterprise Services
> Notary Public Section
> P.O. Box 452
> Trenton, NJ 08646

Change of Name

Notification Required. When a Notary changes his or her name, notification must be made to the State Treasurer — and all county clerks where additional certificates may have been filed — before notarizing any documents.

Change of name forms are available at *www.state.nj.us/treasury/revenue/notarychange.pdf* or by calling (609) 292-9292.

The Notary must return the change of name form and a $25 fee (payable to the State Treasurer) by certified mail to the Notary Public Section at the address above. Once a name change form has been filed, the Notary must notarize using the new name (NJSA 52:7-18).

Commission Certificate. A New Jersey Notary who files a change of name form with the State Treasurer also may request a new commission certificate indicating the new name, though this is not required.

The request should be made when filing the name change form and must be accompanied by a $1 fee, in addition to the $25 fee for filing the name change.

OFFICIAL NOTARIAL ACTS

Authorized Acts

Notaries may perform the following official acts:

- Acknowledgments, certifying that a signer personally appeared before the Notary, was identified by the Notary, and acknowledged freely signing the document (NJSA 46:14-6.1; see pages 9–11).

- Depositions, taking down in writing the spoken words of a person giving testimony, though this act is most often done by skilled court reporters (NJ Rules of Civil Procedure, Rule 4:12, Section 4:12-1; see pages 12–13).

- Affidavits, involving the administration of an oath or affirmation in conjunction with a person's signed statement (NJSA 41:2-17; see pages 11–12).

- Jurats, as found in affidavits and other sworn documents, certifying that the signer personally appeared before the Notary, was identified by the Notary, signed in the Notary's presence, and took an oath or affirmation from the Notary (NJSA 41:2-17; see pages 13–14).

- Oaths and Affirmations, which are solemn promises to a Supreme Being (oath) or solemn promises on one's own personal honor (affirmation) (NJSA 41:2-1, 41:2-17; see pages 15–17).

- Proofs of Execution, certifying that a subscribing witness personally appeared and swore to the Notary that another person, the principal (the signer named in the document), signed that document (NJSA 46:14-6.1; see pages 17–19).

- Protests, certifying that a written promise to pay, such as a bill of exchange, was not honored (NJSA 2A:82-7; see pages 19–21).

- Witnessing a Safe Deposit Box Opening, by a bank or other safe deposit box owner, and certifying related details (NJSA 17:14A-51; see pages 21–21).

Unauthorized Acts

Certified Copies. A certified copy is a verified exact duplicate of an original document. A New Jersey Notary is not expressly authorized by law to issue certified copies.

Requests for certified copies should be directed to the agency that holds or issued the original. For certified copies of birth, death, or marriage certificates, and other vital records, the person requesting the copy should be referred to the Bureau of Vital Statistics (or the equivalent) in the state where the event occurred.

In states that do not authorize Notaries to certify copies, Notaries may notarize a signed, written declaration made by the owner or holder of a document that a copy is a true copy of the original. This process is commonly called "copy certification by document custodian" and may serve as an acceptable alternative to a Notary-certified copy. The receiving party determines if this alternative is acceptable. The requesting person, not the Notary, should provide the declaration and specify the notarial act to be performed if a Notary certificate is not already provided on the declaration. Notaries should be careful not to guide the process or to make any recommendations or claims concerning the legality or sufficiency of this alternative.

Marriages. New Jersey Notaries have no authority to perform marriages unless they are also ministers. Only Notaries in Florida, Maine, Nevada, and South Carolina are empowered to perform marriages strictly by virtue of holding a Notary commission.

Acknowledgments

Definition. An acknowledgment is a notarial act in which a document signer personally appears before a Notary, is identified by the Notary as the person named in the document, and admits (or "acknowledges") to the Notary that he or she signed the document for the purposes stated in it.

The signer may be signing as an individual, acting on his or her own behalf, or in a representative capacity, acting on behalf of an entity or another person. When a signer is acting in a representative capacity, the signer also acknowledges that he or she has the proper authority to do so (NJSA 46:14-2.1).

Purpose. Acknowledgments are one of the most common forms of notarization. Typically, they are executed on deeds and other documents that will be publicly recorded by a county official (NJSA 46:14-2.1). The primary purpose of an acknowledgment is to positively identify the document signer.

Procedure. In executing an acknowledgment, a Notary certifies three things (NJSA 46:14-2.1):

- The signer *personally appeared* before the Notary on the date and in the county indicated on the Notary certificate.

- The signer was *positively identified* by the Notary through either personal knowledge or satisfactory evidence (see "Identifying Document Signers," pages 22–26).

- The signer *acknowledged* to the Notary that the signature is his or hers and was freely made for the purposes stated in the document. If the document is signed in a representative capacity, the signer also acknowledged that he or she had the proper authority to do so. (If a document is willingly signed in the presence of the Notary, this act can serve just as well as an oral statement of acknowledgment.)

Identification of Acknowledger. In executing an acknowledgment, the Notary must identify the signer through personal knowledge, a credible identifying witness or identification documents. (See "Identifying Document Signers," pages 22–26.)

Witnessing Signature Not Required. For an acknowledgment, the document does not have to be signed in the Notary's presence; however, the signer must appear before the Notary at the time of notarization to acknowledge having signed the document (NJSA 46:14-2.1).

A document could have been signed an hour before, a week before, a year before, etc. — as long as the signer appears before the Notary with the signed document at the time of notarization to admit that the signature is his or her own.

Representative Capacity. When the signer is signing in a representative capacity — that is, on behalf of another person or of a legal entity such as a corporation or partnership — the signer does not need to produce proof of his or her capacity. The signer must, however, verbally acknowledge that he or she has the legal authority to sign on behalf of the other person or the entity (NJSA 46:14-2.1).

Certificate for Acknowledgment. For every acknowledgment, the Notary must complete, sign and seal (if a seal is used) an appropriate certificate of acknowledgment (NJSA 46:14-2.1).

The certificate wording may either be preprinted or typed at the end of the document, or appear as an attachment (a "loose certificate") that is stapled to the document's signature page (NJSA 2A:82-17, 46:14-2.1).

Unlike most states, New Jersey statutes do not prescribe acknowledgment certificate wording that Notaries must use. However, the online edition of the *New Jersey Notary Public Manual* offers an example of an acknowledgment certificate with basic wording, not prohibiting use of any other appropriate wording:

State of New Jersey   )
) ss.
County of _____   )

On _____, 20___, before me, _____, a Notary Public in and for said county, personally appeared _____ (name[s] of signer[s]), who has/have satisfactorily identified himself/herself/themselves as the signer(s) or/witness(es) to the above-referenced document.

Notary Signature _____   (Notary's Seal)

Affidavits

Definition. An affidavit is a signed statement made under oath or affirmation before a Notary or other oath-administering official. The signer of an affidavit is called an affiant.

When taking an affidavit, the Notary must administer the oath or affirmation to the affiant and then complete some form of jurat — the name of the Notary wording for affidavits, depositions, and other sworn statements. (See "Jurats," pages 13–14.)

Purpose. Affidavits are used in and out of court for a variety of purposes, from declaring losses to an insurance company to declaring U.S. citizenship before traveling to a foreign country. If an affidavit is used in a judicial proceeding, only one side in the lawsuit or court case need participate in the execution of the affidavit.

Wording for Affidavit Oath (Affirmation). If no other wording is prescribed in a given instance, a Notary may use the following language in administering an oath (or affirmation) to an affiant:

> Do you solemnly swear that the statements in this document are true to the best of your knowledge and belief, so help you God?
>
> (Do you solemnly affirm that the statements in this document are true to the best of your knowledge and belief?)

For both oath and affirmation, the affiant must respond aloud and affirmatively, with "I do" or similar words. It is traditional for the Notary and the affiant to raise their right hands during the oath or affirmation.

Certificate. Affidavits require jurat certificates in some form. (See "Jurats," pages 13–14.)

Depositions

Definition. A deposition is a written transcript of a person's oral statements, which the person then signs and swears to or affirms before a Notary or other oath-administering official. The signer of a deposition is called a deponent.

When taking a deposition, the Notary must administer the oath or affirmation to the deponent and then complete some form of jurat — the name of the Notary wording for affidavits, depositions, and other sworn statements. (See "Jurats," pages 13–14.)

Purpose. Unlike affidavits, depositions are used only in judicial proceedings. With a deposition, both sides in a lawsuit or court case typically have the opportunity to cross-examine the deponent. Their questions and the deponent's answers are taken down and then transcribed into a written statement.

Procedure. New Jersey law permits any Notary to take a deposition — that is, to transcribe the words spoken aloud by a deponent (NJSA 41:2-1, 41:2-17). This duty, however, is most often executed by Notaries who are trained and certified shorthand reporters, also known as court reporters.

While most Notaries do not have the stenographic skills necessary to transcribe a deponent's words, any Notary is competent to administer an oath or affirmation or to execute a jurat for a deposition.

Wording for Deposition Oath (Affirmation). If no other wording is prescribed in a given instance, a Notary may use the following language in administering an oath (or affirmation) to a deponent:

> Do you solemnly swear that the statements in this document are true to the best of your knowledge and belief, so help you God?
>
> (Do you solemnly affirm that the statements in this document are true to the best of your knowledge and belief?)

For both oath and affirmation, the deponent must respond aloud and affirmatively, with "I do" or similar words. It is traditional for the Notary and the deponent to raise their right hands during the oath or affirmation.

Certificate. Depositions require jurat certificates in some form. (See "Jurats," pages 13–14.)

Jurats

Definition. A jurat is a notarial act in which a document signer personally appears before a Notary, is identified by the Notary, signs his or her statement in front of the Notary, and swears or affirms to the Notary that the contents of the statement are true.

Purpose. When notarizing affidavits, depositions, and other forms of written verification requiring the signer to take an oath or affirmation, the Notary normally executes a jurat. While the purpose of an acknowledgment is to positively identify a document signer, the purpose of a jurat is to compel truthfulness by appealing to the signer's conscience and fear of criminal penalties for perjury.

Procedure. In executing a jurat, a Notary certifies four things:

- The signer *personally appeared* before the Notary on the date and in the county indicated on the certificate.

- The signer was *positively identified* by the Notary through either personal knowledge or satisfactory evidence (see "Identifying Document Signers," page 22–26).

- The Notary *witnessed the signer sign the document* at the time of notarization.

- The Notary *administered an oath or affirmation* to the signer.

A Notary Public does not execute a jurat by merely asking a person whether or not the signature on an affidavit is that of the signer. An oath or affirmation must be administered and the affixation of the signature observed by the Notary (NJSA 41:2-17).

Identification. In executing a jurat, the Notary must identify the signer through personal knowledge, a credible identifying witness, or identification documents. (See "Identifying Document Signers," pages 22–26.)

Wording for Jurat Oath (Affirmation). If not otherwise prescribed by law, a New Jersey Notary may use the following or similar words to administer an oath (or affirmation) in conjunction with a jurat:

> Do you solemnly swear that the statements in this document are true to the best of your knowledge and belief, so help you God?
>
> (Do you solemnly affirm that the statements in this document are true to the best of your knowledge and belief?)

For both oath and affirmation, the signer must respond aloud and affirmatively, with "I do" or similar words. It is traditional for the Notary and the signer to raise their right hands during the oath or affirmation.

Certificate for Jurat. After administering the oath or affirmation, the Notary must complete a jurat certificate. Typical jurat wording is, "Subscribed and sworn to (or affirmed) before me on this (date) by (name of signer)..." or similar language. "Subscribed" means "signed."

When jurat wording is not prescribed in a given instance, the National Notary Association recommends the following:

State of New Jersey   )
) ss.
County of _____   )

Subscribed and sworn to (or affirmed) before me this _____ day of _____ (month), _____ (year), by _____ (name of signer).

(Notary's Signature) _____   (Notary's Seal)

Oaths and Affirmations

Definition. An oath is a solemn, spoken pledge to a Supreme Being. An affirmation is a solemn, spoken pledge on one's own personal honor, with no reference to a Supreme Being. Both are usually a promise of truthfulness or fidelity and have the same legal effect.

Purpose. In taking an oath or affirmation in an official proceeding, a person may be subject to criminal penalties for perjury should he or she fail to be truthful.

An oath or affirmation can be a full-fledged notarial act in its own right, as when giving an oath of office to a public official, or it can be part of the process of notarizing a document (e.g., executing a jurat, or swearing in a credible identifying witness).

A person who objects to taking an oath — pledging to a Supreme Being — may instead be given an affirmation (NJSA 41:1-6).

Personal Appearance Required. An oath or affirmation may not be given over the telephone. The person taking the oath or affirmation must physically appear in front of the Notary.

Wording for Oaths (Affirmations). If not otherwise prescribed by law, a New Jersey Notary may use the following or similar words to administer an oath (or affirmation):

- Oath (affirmation) for affiant signing an affidavit or deponent signing a deposition:

  Do you solemnly swear that the statements in this document are true to the best of your knowledge and belief, so help you God?

  (Do you solemnly affirm that the statements in this document are true to the best of your knowledge and belief?)

- Oath (affirmation) for credible identifying witness:

  Do you solemnly swear that you know the signer truly is the person he/she claims to be, so help you God?

  (Do you solemnly affirm that you know the signer truly is the person he/she claims to be?)

- Oath (affirmation) for subscribing witness:

  Do you solemnly swear that you saw (name of document signer) sign his/her name to this document and/or that he/she acknowledged to you having executed it for the purposes therein stated, so help you God?

  (Do you solemnly affirm that you saw [name of document signer] sign his/her name to this document and/or that he/she acknowledged to you having executed it for the purposes therein stated?)

Response Required. The oath-taker or affirmant must respond by repeating the wording in the first person — "I solemnly swear ..." — or by answering affirmatively with, "I do," "Yes," or similar words. A nod or grunt is not a clear and sufficient response.

Ceremony and Gestures. To impress upon the oath-taker or affirmant the importance of truthfulness, the Notary is encouraged to lend a sense of ceremony and formality to the oath or affirmation. During administration of the oath or affirmation, the Notary and the person taking the oath or affirmation traditionally raise their right hands, though this is not a legal requirement. Notaries generally have discretion to use words and gestures they feel will most compellingly appeal to the conscience of the oath-taker or affirmant.

Exclusions. Only an individual may take an oath or affirmation. An "artificial person" such as a corporation or a partnership may not take an oath.

In addition, a Notary may not administer an oath or affirmation to himself or herself.

Proof of Execution by Subscribing Witness

Definition. A proof of execution by subscribing witness is a notarial act in which a subscribing witness personally appears before a Notary, is identified by the Notary, and swears or affirms the following facts to the Notary (NJSA 46:14-2.1):

- The subscribing witness personally knows the person named in the document — the absent principal signer, on whose behalf the subscribing witness is appearing.

- The subscribing witness watched the principal willingly sign ("execute") the document or personally took the principal's acknowledgment of having willingly signed.

- At the request of the principal, the subscribing witness signed ("subscribed") his or her own name to the document as a witness to its execution.

- The subscribing witness's signature and sworn testimony are accepted as the "proof" of the document's execution by the absent principal signer.

Purpose. In executing a proof of execution by subscribing witness, a Notary certifies that the signature of a person who does not appear before the Notary — the principal signer — is genuine and was freely made, based on the sworn testimony of another person who does appear — a subscribing (signing) witness (NJSA 46:14-2.1).

Proofs of execution are used when the principal signer is out of town or otherwise unavailable to appear before a Notary. Because of their high potential for fraudulent abuse, proofs of execution are not universally accepted, though they are legal for the New Jersey Notary to perform.

That said, New Jersey state officials discourage the use of proofs of execution by subscribing witness. This type of notarization should only be used as a last resort and never merely because the principal signer prefers not to take the time to personally appear before a Notary.

In Lieu of Acknowledgment. On recordable documents, a proof of execution by subscribing witness is usually regarded as an acceptable substitute for an acknowledgment.

NEW JERSEY NOTARY LAW PRIMER

<u>Identifying Subscribing Witness</u>. Since the Notary is relying entirely on the word of the subscribing witness to vouch for an absent signer's identity, willingness to sign, and general awareness, it is best for subscribing witnesses to be personally known to the Notary, and this is strongly recommended by Notary regulators.

New Jersey law does not indicate the means by which a subscribing witness may be identified. The certificate wording provided in the *New Jersey Notary Public Manual* for a proof of execution indicates that either the Notary's personal knowledge or the sworn word of a credible identifying witness is acceptable. Identification documents (ID cards) do not appear to be an option.

<u>Subscribing Witness Qualifications</u>. The ideal subscribing witness personally knows the principal signer and has no personal beneficial or financial interest in the document or transaction. It would be foolish of the Notary, for example, to rely on the word of a subscribing witness presenting for notarization a power of attorney naming that very witness as attorney in fact.

<u>Oath (Affirmation) for Subscribing Witness</u>. An acceptable oath (or affirmation) for the subscribing witness might be:

> Do you solemnly swear that you saw (name of the document signer) sign his/her name to this document and/or that he/she acknowledged to you having executed it for the purposes therein stated, so help you God?
>
> (Do you solemnly affirm that you saw [name of the document signer] sign his/her name to this document and/or that he/she acknowledged to you having executed it for the purposes therein stated?)

<u>Certificate for Proof of Execution</u>. New Jersey statute does not prescribe a Notary certificate for a proof of execution by subscribing witness, though it does specify that the witness must swear that he or she saw the principal signer execute the document (NJSA 46:14-2.1). The *New Jersey Notary Public Manual* prescribes the following certificate for a proof of execution by subscribing witness:

> State of New Jersey   )
>   ) ss.
> County of _____   )
>
> On _____ (date), before me, _____, Notary Public in and for said county, personally appeared _____ (name[s] of subscribing witness[es]), personally known to me (or proved to me on the oath of

_____ [name of credible identifying witness]) to be the person(s) whose name(s) is/are subscribed on the attached document as witness(es) thereto, and who, being duly sworn by me, say(s) that he/she/they saw _____ (name of absent principal) sign the attached document, and that said affiant(s) subscribed his/her/their name(s) to the attached document at the request of _____ (name of absent principal).

Notary's Signature _____   (Notary's Seal)

Protests

Definition. A protest is a written statement by a Notary or other authorized officer, verifying that payment was not received on a negotiable instrument such as a bank draft. Failure to pay is called dishonor.

Before issuing a certificate of protest, the Notary must present the bank draft or other instrument to the person or entity obligated to pay, a procedure called presentment (NJSA 2A:82-7).

Purpose. The purpose of a protest is to evidence the dishonor of a negotiable instrument. The protest initiates the civil process of recovering the payment that was dishonored.

Protest of instruments held by a bank or corporation by a Notary officer or employee is permitted (NJSA 7:5-6).

Antiquated Act. In the 19th century, protests were common notarial acts in the United States, but they are rarely performed today due to the advent of modern electronic communications and resulting changes in our banking and financial systems. Modern Notaries most often encounter protests in the context of international commerce.

Special Knowledge Required. Notarial acts of protest are complicated and varied, requiring a special knowledge of financial and legal terminology. Only Notaries who have the requisite knowledge, or who are acting under the supervision of an experienced bank officer or an attorney familiar with the Uniform Commercial Code, should attempt a protest.

Notary's Record of Protests Required. When protesting any bill of exchange or promissory note, Notaries must record certain information in a recordbook or journal.

For all demands of payment, the Notary must record:

- The date and time the demand was made.
- The place where the demand was made.
- The name of the person to whom the demand was made.

For all notices of nonpayment served, the Notary must record:

- If the notice was served in person:
  - The manner in which it was served.
  - The date and time it was served.
- If the notice was sent by means other than post:
  - The manner in which it was sent.
  - The date and time it was sent.
- If the notice was sent by post:
  - The name of the person to whom it was mailed.
  - The address to which it was mailed.
  - The date and time it was mailed

Finally, the Notary must sign this record in the recordbook or journal and must keep a copy of all notices of nonpayment (NJSA 7:5-3).

<u>Certificate for Protest</u>. A Notary must provide a certificate to the person requesting a protest. The certificate should include the following information (NJSA 7:5-3, 7:5-4):

- The time and place of presentment of the bill or note.
- The name of the party to whom demand of payment was made.
- A copy of the notice of nonpayment, including how, when and where it was served.

Notary's Record of Protests Required. Every Notary Public, upon protesting any bill of exchange or promissory note, must record in a recordbook the time, place and name of the person upon whom demand of payment was made, with a copy of the notice of nonpayment, how and when served; or if sent, in what manner and the time when. If sent by mail, the record must include to whom presentment was directed, the address, and when the notice was deposited at the post office. The Notary's signature must also be on the record (NJSA 7:5-3).

Witnessing Safe Deposit Box Opening

Purpose. If the rental fee on a safe deposit box, vault, or receptacle has not been paid for one year, and the bank or safe deposit box owner has attempted to contact the lessee without success, the bank may open and inventory the box in the presence of a Notary Public and one of the institution's officers.

Procedure. The Notary issues a certificate stating the lessee's name, the date of the opening, and a list of the contents in the box. The Notary then delivers the certificate to the institution. Within 10 days of the opening, a copy of the certificate must be mailed by the owner of the safe deposit box to the lessee's last known address (NJSA 17:14A-51).

Certificate for Inventorying a Safe Deposit Box. New Jersey law does not provide specific wording for the certificate. The National Notary Association recommends the following wording:

State of New Jersey)
) ss.
County of _____)

On the _____ (day) of _____ (month), _____ (year), safe deposit box number _____, rented in the name of _____, was opened by _____ (name of financial institution) in my presence and in the presence of _____ (name of financial institution officer). The contents of the box consisted of the following: (list of contents)

_____ (Signature of financial institution officer)
_____ (Print or type name)
_____ (Signature of Notary)   (Notary's Seal)
_____ (Name of Notary, printed, typed or stamped)

PRACTICES AND PROCEDURES

Personal Appearance

Required. New Jersey law expressly requires document signers to personally appear before the Notary at the time of notarization (NJSA 46:14-2.1). This means that the Notary and the signer must both be physically present, face to face in the same room, when the notarization takes place. Notarizations may never be performed over the telephone.

Willingness

Confirmation. New Jersey Notaries are required to confirm that the signer is signing willingly (*New Jersey Notary Public Manual*).

To confirm willingness, the Notary need only ask document signers if they are signing of their own free will. If a signer does or says anything that makes the Notary think the signer is being pressured to sign, the Notary must refuse to notarize.

Awareness

Confirmation. New Jersey Notaries are required to confirm that the signer is aware of what he or she is signing (*New Jersey Notary Public Manual*).

To confirm awareness, the Notary simply makes a layperson's judgment about the signer's ability to understand what he or she is signing. A document signer who cannot respond intelligibly in a simple conversation with the Notary should not be considered sufficiently aware to sign at that moment. If the notarization is taking place in a medical environment, the signer's doctor can be consulted for a professional opinion. Otherwise, if the signer's awareness is in doubt, the Notary must refuse to notarize.

Identifying Document Signers

Required. In taking the acknowledgment of a signature on any document, New Jersey Notaries are required by law to identify the person making the acknowledgment (NJSA 46:14-2.1). The *New Jersey Notary Public Manual* stipulates that Notaries must identify *all* signers, regardless of the type of notarial act.

Three Identification Methods. The following three methods of identification are generally acceptable:

- The Notary's personal knowledge of the signer's identity (see "Personal Knowledge of Identity," page 23)

- The oath or affirmation of a personally known credible identifying witness (see "Credible Identifying Witnesses," pages 23–24)

- Reliable identification documents or ID cards (see "Identification Documents," pages 24–26)

Personal Knowledge of Identity

Definition. The safest and most reliable method of identifying a document signer is for the Notary to depend on his or her own personal knowledge of the signer's identity. Personal knowledge means familiarity with an individual resulting from interactions with that person over a period of time sufficient to eliminate any reasonable doubt that the person has the identity claimed. The familiarity should come from association with the individual in relation to other people and should be based upon a chain of circumstances surrounding the individual.

New Jersey law does not specify how long a Notary must be acquainted with an individual before personal knowledge of identity may be claimed. The Notary's common sense must prevail. In general, the longer the Notary is acquainted with a person, and the more interactions the Notary has had with that person, the more likely the individual is indeed personally known.

For instance, the Notary might safely regard a friend since childhood as personally known, but the Notary would be foolish to consider a person met for the first time the previous day as such. Whenever the Notary has a reasonable doubt about a signer's identity, that individual should be considered not personally known, and the identification should be made through other acceptable methods: either a credible identifying witness or reliable identification documents.

Credible Identifying Witnesses

Purpose. When a document signer is not personally known to the Notary and is not able to present reliable ID cards, that signer may be identified on the oath or affirmation of a credible identifying witness. This procedure is considered to provide "satisfactory evidence" of the signer's identity.

Qualifications. Every credible identifying witness must personally know the document signer. The credible identifying witness also must be personally known by the Notary. This establishes a "chain of personal knowledge" from the Notary to the credible identifying witness to the signer. In a sense, a credible identifying witness is a walking, talking ID card.

A credible identifying witness should have a reputation for honesty. The witness should be a competent, independent individual who won't be tricked, cajoled, bullied, or otherwise influenced into identifying someone he or she does not really know. In addition, the witness should have no direct personal interest in the transaction requiring a notarial act.

Oath (Affirmation) for Credible Identifying Witness. The Notary must administer an oath or affirmation to the credible identifying witness in order to compel truthfulness.

If not otherwise prescribed by law, the following or similar wording may be used by a New Jersey Notary:

> Do you solemnly swear that you know the signer truly is the person he/she claims to be, so help you God?
>
> (Do you solemnly affirm that you know the signer truly is the person he/she claims to be?)

Journal Entry. If the Notary maintains a journal, each credible identifying witness should sign the Notary's journal in the place where the Notary indicates the method of identification of the signer. The Notary should also print each witness's name and address.

Not a Subscribing Witness. Notaries must not confuse a credible identifying witness with a subscribing witness. A credible identifying witness vouches for the identity of a signer who appears before the Notary. A subscribing witness vouches for the genuineness of the signature of a person who does not appear before the Notary. (See "Proof of Execution by Subscribing Witness," pages 17–19.)

Identification Documents (ID Cards)

Acceptable Identification Documents. Notaries customarily are allowed to use reliable identification documents (ID cards) to identify document signers whom they do not personally know. Such cards are considered to be "satisfactory evidence" of the signer's identity.

The National Notary Association urges Notaries to rely only on IDs with a photograph, a physical description (e.g., "brown hair, green eyes"), and a signature of the bearer. Most government-issued IDs contain all three components.

Examples of acceptable forms of identification include:

- New Jersey driver's license or official nondriver's ID.

- U.S. or foreign passport.

- U.S. military ID.

- Permanent resident card, or "green card," issued by the U.S. Citizenship and Immigration Services (USCIS).

Multiple Identification. While one good identification document or card may be sufficient to identify a signer, the Notary may always ask for more, especially if the Notary has reasons to suspect that the signer has presented fraudulent identification.

Unacceptable Identification Documents. Because they are easily counterfeited, Social Security cards, birth certificates, and credit cards are worthless as primary identifying documents.

Name Variations. The Notary must make sure that the name on the document is the same as the name appearing on the identification presented.

In certain circumstances, it may be acceptable for the name on the document to be an abbreviated form of the name on the ID — for example, John D. Smith instead of John David Smith. Last names or surnames, however, should always be the same.

Fraudulent Identification. Identification documents are the least secure of the three methods of identifying a document signer, because phony ID cards are common. The Notary should scrutinize each card for evidence of tampering or counterfeiting, or for evidence that it is a genuine card that has been issued to an impostor.

Some clues that an ID card may have been fraudulently altered include mismatched type styles, a photograph with a raised surface, a signature that does not match the signature on the document, unauthorized lamination of the card, and smudges, erasures, smears and discolorations.

Possible tip-offs to a counterfeit ID card include misspelled words, a brand new-looking card with an old date of issuance, two cards with exactly the same photograph showing the bearer in identical clothing or with an identical background, and inappropriate patterns and features.

Indications that an identification card may have been issued to an impostor include the birthdate or address on the card being unfamiliar to the bearer and all the ID cards seeming brand new.

Journal of Notarial Acts

Recommended. New Jersey law specifically requires Notaries to maintain a record of protests, including all pertinent information relating to their execution (NJSA 7:5-3). However, since New Jersey statute also stipulates that each Notary must take an oath of office swearing "that he will make and keep a true record of all such matters as are required by law" (NJSA 52:7-14), the National Notary Association recommends that each Notary maintain a recordbook or official Notary journal chronicling *all* notarial acts.

Purpose. Prudent Notaries keep detailed and accurate journals of their notarial acts for many reasons:

- Keeping records is a *businesslike practice* that every conscientious businessperson and public official should engage in. Not keeping records of important transactions, whether private or public, is risky.

- A Notary's recordbook *protects the public's rights* to valuable property and to due process by providing documentary evidence in the event a document is lost or altered, or if a transaction is later challenged.

- In the event of a civil lawsuit alleging that the Notary's negligence or misconduct caused the plaintiff serious financial harm, a detailed journal of notarial acts can *protect the Notary* by showing that reasonable care was used to identify a signer. It would be difficult to contend that the Notary did not bother to identify a signer if the Notary's journal contains a detailed description of the ID cards that the signer presented.

- Since civil lawsuits arising from a contested notarial act typically occur three to six years after the act occurs, the

Notary normally cannot accurately testify in court about the particulars of a notarization without a journal to *aid the Notary's memory*.

- Journals of notarial acts *prevent baseless lawsuits* by showing that a Notary did use reasonable care, or that a transaction did occur as recorded. Journal thumbprints and signatures are especially effective in defeating such groundless suits.

- Requiring each document signer to leave a signature — or even a thumbprint — in the Notary's journal both *deters attempted forgeries* and provides strong evidence for a conviction should a forgery occur.

Journal Entries. The Notary's journal should contain the following information for each notarial act performed:

- The date, time of day, and type of notarization (e.g., jurat, acknowledgment, etc.)

- The type (or title) of document notarized, including the number of pages and the date of the document

- The signature, address, and printed name of each document signer and witness

- A statement as to how the signer's identity was confirmed

  - If the signer was identified by personal knowledge, the journal entry should read "personal knowledge."

  - If the signer was identified by identification document, the journal entry should contain a description of the ID card accepted, including the type of ID, the government agency issuing the ID, the serial or identifying number of the ID, and its date of issuance or expiration.

  - If the signer was identified by a credible identifying witness, the journal entry should contain the signature, name, and address of the witness.

- Any other pertinent information, including the fee charged for the Notary service or any peculiarities relating to the signer or the document

Document Dates. If the document has a specific date on it, the Notary should record that date in the journal of notarial acts.

Often the only date on a document is the date of the signature that is being notarized. If the signature is undated, however, the document may have no date on it at all. In that case, the Notary should record "no date" or "undated" in the journal.

For acknowledgments, the date the document was signed must either precede or be the same as the date of the notarization; it may not follow it. For a jurat, the date the document was signed and the date of the notarization must be the same.

A document whose signature is dated after the date on its Notary certificate risks rejection by a recorder, who may question how the document could have been notarized before it was signed.

Journal Signature. Perhaps the most important entry to obtain is the signer's signature. A journal signature protects the Notary against claims that a signer did not appear and is a deterrent to forgery, because it provides evidence of the signer's identity and appearance before the Notary.

To check for possible forgery, the Notary should compare the signature that the person leaves in the journal of notarial acts with the signatures on the document and on the IDs. The signatures should be at least reasonably similar.

The Notary also should observe the signing of the journal. If the signer appears to be laboring over the journal signature, this may be an indication of forgery in progress.

Since a journal signature is not required by law, the Notary may not refuse to notarize if the signer declines to leave one.

Journal Thumbprint. Many Notaries are asking document signers to leave a thumbprint in the journal. The journal thumbprint protects the Notary against claims that a signer did not appear and is a strong deterrent to forgery, because it represents absolute proof of the signer's identity and appearance before the Notary.

Provided the signer is willing, nothing prevents a Notary from asking for a thumbprint for every notarial act. Since a thumbprint is not required by law, however, the Notary may not refuse to notarize if the signer declines to leave one.

Additional Entries. Notaries may include additional information in the journal that is pertinent to a given notarization. Many Notaries, for example, enter the telephone number of all signers and witnesses, as well as the address where the notarization was performed, if not at the Notary's office. A description of the document signer's demeanor (e.g., "The signer appeared very nervous") or notations about the identity of other persons who were present for the notarization may also be pertinent.

One important entry to include is the signer's representative capacity — whether the signer is acting as attorney in fact, trustee, guardian, corporate officer, or in another capacity — if not signing on his or her own behalf.

Complete Entry Before Certificate. The prudent Notary completes the journal entry before filling out the Notary certificate on a document. This prevents the signer from leaving with the notarized document before vital information can be entered in the journal.

Never Surrender Journal. Notaries should never surrender control of their journals to anyone, unless expressly subpoenaed by a court order. Even when an employer has paid for the Notary's official journal, it goes with the Notary upon termination of employment.

No person but the Notary may properly possess and use this official tool of the Notary's office. This also means that a Notary may never share his or her journal with another person, even if the other person also is a Notary.

Notary Certificate

Definition. The Notary certificate is wording that indicates exactly what the Notary has certified or attested to in a particular notarization.

Requirement. When notarizing any document, a Notary must complete a Notary certificate.

Format. The Notary certificate either may be preprinted or typed on the document itself or may be an attachment to it. The certificate should contain (NJSA 2A:82-17, 46:14-2.1):

- A *venue* indicating where the notarization is being performed. "State of New Jersey, County of _____," is the typical venue wording, with the county name inserted in the blank. The letters "SS." or "SCT." sometimes appear after the venue; they abbreviate the traditional Latin word *scilicet*, meaning "in particular" or "namely."

- A *statement of particulars,* which indicates what the notarization has attested. An acknowledgment certificate might include such wording as: "On _____ (date) before me, _____ (name of Notary), personally appeared _____ (name of signer), personally known to me (or proved to me on the basis of satisfactory evidence) to be the person(s)..." etc. A jurat certificate would include such wording as: "Subscribed and sworn to (or affirmed) before me this _____ (date) by _____ (name of signer)."

- A *testimonium clause*, which may be optional if the date is included in the statement of particulars: "Witness my hand and official seal, this the ____ day of _____ (month), ____ (year)." In this short sentence, the Notary formally attests to the truthfulness of the preceding facts in the certificate. "Hand" means signature.

- The *official signature of the Notary*, exactly as the name appears on the Notary's commission certificate.

- The *official seal of the Notary*, although not required by New Jersey law, placed near but not over the Notary's signature.

New Jersey also requires Notaries to print, type or stamp their name (NJSA 52:7-19) and commission expiration date (*New Jersey Notary Public Manual*) on every Notary certificate.

Completing the Certificate. When filling in the blanks in the Notary certificate, Notaries should either type or print neatly in dark ink.

Notaries also must pay attention to places on the Notary certificate that indicate the number and gender of the document signers, as well as how they were identified — for example, leave the plural "(s)" untouched or cross it out, as appropriate.

Correcting a Certificate. When filling out the certificate, the Notary needs to make sure any preprinted information is accurate.

For example, the venue — the state and county in which the notarial act is taking place — may have been filled in prior to the notarization. If the preprinted venue is incorrect, the Notary must line through the incorrect state and/or county, write in the proper site of the notarization, and initial and date the change.

Loose Certificates. When certificate wording is not preprinted on the document, or when preprinted wording is not acceptable, the Notary may attach a loose certificate. This form typically is stapled to the document's left margin following the signature page.

If the loose certificate is replacing unacceptable preprinted wording, the Notary should line through the preprinted wording and write below it, "See attached certificate." If the document has no preprinted wording, however, the Notary should not add this notation. Those words could be viewed as an unauthorized change to the document.

To prevent a loose certificate from being removed and fraudulently placed on another document, the Notary may add a brief description of the document to the certificate: "This certificate is attached to a _____ (title or type of document), dated _____ (date), of _____ (number) pages, signed by _____ (name[s] of signer[s])." The National Notary Association offers loose certificates that have similar wording preprinted on them; otherwise, the Notary will have to print, type, or stamp this information on each loose certificate used.

Finally, when Notaries attach a loose certificate to a document, they always should note in their journals that they did so, as well as the means by which they attached the certificate to the document: "Loose certificate stapled to document, following signature page."

While fraud-deterrent steps such as these can make it much more difficult for a loose certificate to be removed and misused, there is no absolute protection against its removal and misuse. While a loose certificate remains in their control, however, Notaries must absolutely ensure that it is attached only to its intended document.

Selecting Certificates. Nonattorney Notaries should never select Notary certificates for any transaction. It is not the role of a nonattorney Notary to decide what type of certificate — and thus what type of notarization — a document needs. As ministerial officials, Notaries generally follow instructions and complete forms that have been provided for them; they do not issue instructions or decide which forms are appropriate in a given case.

If a document is presented to a Notary without certificate wording and if the signer does not know what type of notarial act is appropriate, the signer should be asked to find out what kind of notarization and certificate are needed. Usually the agency that issued or will be accepting the document can provide this information. A Notary who selects certificates may be engaging in the unauthorized practice of law.

Do Not Pre-Sign or Pre-Seal Certificates. A Notary must never sign and/or seal certificates ahead of time or permit other persons to attach loose Notary certificates to documents.

A Notary must never give or mail an unattached, signed, and sealed loose certificate to another person and trust that person to attach it to a particular document, even if asked to do so by a signer who previously appeared before the Notary.

These actions could facilitate fraud or forgery, and, since such actions would be indefensible in a civil court of law, they could subject the Notary to lawsuits to recover damages resulting from the Notary's neglect or misconduct.

False Certificates. A Notary who knowingly completes a false Notary certificate may be subject to criminal penalties. A Notary would be completing a false certificate, for example, if he or she signed and sealed an acknowledgment certificate indicating a signer personally appeared when the signer actually did not.

Notaries may be pressured by employers, clients, friends or relatives to be untruthful in their official certificates. If a Notary complies with these requests, he or she may be convicted of a crime of dishonesty. A New Jersey Notary who is convicted of such crimes may lose his or her Notary commission or be denied any future commission. The Notary may also be subject to a civil lawsuit and damages brought by the injured party (NJSA 52:7-20, 52:7-21).

Notary Seal

Optional. New Jersey law does not require Notaries to use seals of office (NJSA 41:1-7, 52:7-19). However, many Notaries elect to use an inking or embossing seal to impart an appropriate sense of ceremony to their official acts.

Another reason for using a Notary seal on notarized documents is that, if the document is sent to another state within the United Sates or to a foreign nation, the absence of a seal may delay or, on occasion in foreign nations, even prevent the document's acceptance.

NOTARY LAWS EXPLAINED

Embossing and Inking Seals. There are two types of Notary seals: the metal embosser, which crimps its impression onto a paper surface and aids in distinguishing photocopies from originals; and the inked stamp, usually with a rubber face, which imprints a photocopiable impression on the paper. Many New Jersey Notaries use rubber stamps to affix their name, commission expiration date and other pertinent information. (See "Required Information," below.)

In many states, county recording officials prefer inking seals because they considerably simplify the process of microfilming property deeds and other recordable documents. Recorders have to smudge seal embossments with carbon or other photocopiable substances before they can be microfilmed.

Required Information. On every certificate, Notaries must print, type, or stamp their name in such a manner that the State Treasurer is able to read the name clearly (NJSA 52:7-19). They also must print, type, or stamp their commission expiration date (*New Jersey Notary Public Manual*).

The Notary may add this information by using an inking seal. The National Notary Association recommends that the Notary also include the words "Notary Public" and any other pertinent information — perhaps the name of the county in which the Notary has filed his or her oath of office — in the seal.

Placement of Seal Impression. The Notary's official seal impression should be affixed near but not over the Notary's signature on the Notary certificate. The Notary should avoid affixing the seal over any text on the document or certificate. This is especially important if the information in the seal will be obscured or if the document will be submitted to a public recorder. Some recorders will reject documents if writing or document text intrudes within the borders of the Notary's seal.

If there is no room for a seal, the Notary may have no choice but to complete and attach a loose certificate that duplicates the Notary wording on the document.

L.S. On many certificates the letters "L.S." appear, indicating where the seal is to be located. These letters abbreviate the Latin term *locus sigilli*, meaning "place of the seal." An inking seal should be placed near but not over the letters, so that wording imprinted by the seal will not be obscured. An embossing seal may be placed directly over the letters, slightly displacing portions of the characters and leaving a clue that document examiners can use to distinguish an original from a forged photocopy.

Illegible Seal. If an initial seal impression is unreadable and there is ample room on the document, another impression can be affixed nearby. The illegibility of the first impression will indicate why a second seal impression was necessary. The Notary should then record in the journal that a second impression was applied.

A Notary should never attempt to fix an imperfect seal impression with pen, ink or correction fluid. This may be viewed as evidence of tampering and cause the document to be rejected by a receiving agency.

Never Surrender Seal. Notaries should never surrender control of their seals to anyone. Even when an employer has paid for the Notary's official seal, it goes with the Notary upon termination of employment.

No person but the Notary may properly possess and use this official tool of the Notary's office. This also means that a Notary may not share his or her seal with another person, even if the other person also is a Notary.

Fees for Notary Services

Maximum Fees. The following maximum fees for performing notarial acts are allowed by New Jersey law (NJSA 22A:4-13, 22A:4-14):

- Acknowledgments — $2.50. For taking an acknowledgment, the fee is not to exceed $2.50 per signature.

- Oaths and Affirmations — $2.50. For administering an oath or affirmation or taking an affidavit, with or without a jurat certificate, the fee is not to exceed $2.50 per person or signer.

- Jurats — $2.50. For executing a jurat with an oath or affirmation, the fee is not to exceed the fee allowed for an oath or affidavit, $2.50 per signer.

- Proofs of Execution by Subscribing Witness — $2.50. For taking a proof of execution by subscribing witness, the maximum fee is the same as for an acknowledgment, $2.50 per signature.

- Real Estate Transfer. In performing any of the above notarizations for a real estate transfer, regardless of the number of notarizations performed in the transaction, a Notary may charge $15.

- Financing of Real Estate. In performing notarizations for mortgagors in the financing of a real estate transaction, regardless of the number of notarizations performed in the transaction, a Notary may charge $25.

- Protests — $2. For executing a protest, the fee is not to exceed $2. For each additional notice of protest delivered in person or by mail, a Notary may charge $0.10 in addition to postage fees.

Travel Fees. Charges for travel by a Notary are not specified by law. Such fees are allowed only if the Notary and signer agree beforehand on the amount to be charged. The signer must understand that a travel fee is not stipulated in law and is separate from the Notary fees described above.

Option Not to Charge. Notaries are not required to charge for their Notary services, and they may charge any fee less than the maximum.

Overcharging. For charging more than the legally prescribed fees in executing a protest, a court may demand a Notary pay $25 for each violation to the person overcharged (NJSA 22A:4-13).
Although the laws only prescribe penalties for protests, charging more than the maximum statutory fee for any notarial act may subject the Notary to penalties or charges of discrimination.

Photocopies & Faxes

Original Signature. A photocopy or fax may be notarized as long as the signature on it is original, meaning that the photocopy or fax must have been signed with pen and ink. Signatures on documents presented for notarization must always be signed with a handwritten, original signature. A photocopied or faxed signature may never be notarized.

Public recorders sometimes will not accept notarized photocopies or faxes, because the text of the document may be too faint to adequately reproduce in microfilming.

Blank or Incomplete Documents

Do Not Notarize. While New Jersey law does not specifically address notarizing a blank or incomplete document, the National Notary Association strongly advises against this practice.

Any blanks in a document should be filled in by the signer prior to notarization. If the blanks are inapplicable and intended to be left unfilled, the signer should line through each space or write "Not Applicable" or "N/A." The Notary may not, however, tell the signer what to write in the blanks. If the signer is unsure how to fill in the blanks, he or she should contact the document's issuer, its eventual recipient, or an attorney.

Disqualifying Interest

Impartiality. Notaries are appointed by the state to be impartial, disinterested witnesses whose screening duties help ensure the integrity of important legal and commercial transactions. Lack of impartiality by a Notary throws doubt on the integrity and lawfulness of any transaction. A Notary should never notarize his or her own signature, or notarize a document to which the Notary is a party or in which the Notary has any financial or beneficial interest.

Financial or Beneficial Interest. A financial or beneficial interest exists when the Notary is individually named as a principal in a financial transaction or when the Notary receives an advantage, right, privilege, property, or fee valued in excess of the lawfully prescribed Notary fee.

In regard to real estate transactions, a Notary usually is considered to have a disqualifying financial or beneficial interest when that Notary is a grantor or grantee, a mortgagor or mortgagee, a trustor or trustee, a vendor or vendee, a lessor or lessee, or will benefit in any way from the transaction.

Relatives. Although New Jersey state law does not expressly prohibit notarizing for a relative, the National Notary Association and state officials strongly advise against doing so for persons related by blood or marriage. Family matters often involve a financial or other beneficial interest that may not be readily apparent at the time of notarization.

Notarizing for family members also may test the Notary's ability to act impartially. For example, a Notary who is asked to notarize a contract signed by his or her brother might attempt to persuade him to sign or not sign. A sibling is entitled to exert influence, but this is entirely improper for a Notary.

Even if a Notary has no interest in the document and does not attempt to influence the signer, notarizing for a relative could subject the document to a legal challenge if other parties to the transaction allege the Notary could not have acted impartially.

Corporations. A New Jersey Notary who is a stockholder, director, officer, employee, or agent of a bank or other corporation may administer an oath to any other stockholder, director, officer, employee, or agent of the corporation (NJSA 41:2-3).

Refusal of Services

Non-customers. An employer may limit the services of Notary employees to business-related notarizations during hours of employment and exclude services to the general public. Notary-employees may refuse to notarize for noncustomers if their employer has limited their services in this manner.

Discrimination. Notaries should honor all lawful and reasonable requests to notarize. A person's race, age, gender, religion, nationality, ethnicity, lifestyle or political viewpoint is never legitimate cause for refusing to perform a notarial act.

Penalty. Should a Notary refuse to perform a lawfully requested notarial act — other than when restricted by the Notary's employer as described above — the Notary may be subject to charges of discrimination and liable to the injured party for any damages.

Exception. A Notary may refuse to notarize a document if he or she knows that the document is blatantly fraudulent.

Employer/Notary Agreement

Agreement to Limit Notary's Services. A Notary Public employed by a financial institution may agree to follow the employer's direction or policy to not administer oaths except in the course of business. The restriction is limited to the Notary's service during regular business hours and is valid only if the Notary agrees to the policy. In this context, a "financial institution" is specifically defined as a state or federally chartered bank, savings bank, savings and loan association, or credit union (NJSA 41:2-3).

It may be helpful to the Notary to have the agreement in writing to prevent any haggling when limiting these services. If the Notary is challenged, the written agreement may serve as evidence that this is the employer's consistent policy, perhaps protecting the Notary and the employer from charges of discrimination.

Reasonable Care

Responsibility. As public servants, Notaries must act responsibly and exercise reasonable care in the performance of their official duties. If a Notary fails to do so, he or she may be subject to a civil suit to recover financial damages caused by the Notary's error or omission.

In general, reasonable care is the degree of concern and attentiveness that a person of normal intelligence and responsibility would exhibit. If a Notary can show a judge or jury that he or she did everything expected of a reasonable person, the judge or jury may be required by law to find the Notary blameless and not liable for damages.

Complying with all pertinent laws is the first rule of reasonable care for a Notary. If there are no statutory guidelines in a given instance, the Notary should go to extremes to use common sense and prudence.

Unauthorized Practice of Law

Do Not Assist in Legal Matters. A nonattorney Notary may not give legal advice or accept fees for legal advice. As a ministerial official, the nonattorney Notary generally is not permitted to assist a signer in drafting, preparing, selecting, completing, or understanding a document or transaction.

The Notary should not fill in the blank spaces in the text of a document for other persons, tell others what documents they need or how to draft them, nor advise others about the legal sufficiency of a document — and especially not for a fee.

A Notary, of course, may fill in the blanks on the portion of any document containing the Notary certificate. And a Notary, as a private individual, may prepare legal documents that he or she is personally a party to, but the Notary may not notarize his or her own signature on these same documents.

Do Not Determine Notarial Act. A Notary who is not an attorney may not determine the type of notarial act to perform or decide which type of Notary certificate to attach. This is beyond the scope of the Notary's expertise and might be considered the unauthorized practice of law. The Notary should only follow instructions provided by the document, its signer, its issuing or receiving agency, or an attorney.

If a document lacks Notary certificate wording, the Notary must ask the document signer what type of notarization is required. The Notary may then type the appropriate Notary wording on the document or attach a loose certificate. If the signer does not know what type of notarization is required, the issuing or receiving agency should be contacted. This decision is never to be made by the Notary, unless the Notary is also an attorney.

Exceptions. Specially trained, nonattorney Notaries certified or licensed in a particular field (e.g., real estate, insurance, escrow, etc.) may offer advice or prepare documents related to that field only. Paralegals under the supervision of an attorney may give advice about documents in routine legal matters.

Signature by Mark

Mark Serves as Signature. A person who cannot sign his or her name because of illiteracy or a physical disability may instead use a mark — an "X", for example — as a signature (NJSA 46:14-4.2).

Witnesses. For a signature by mark to be notarized, the National Notary Association recommends that there be two witnesses to the making of the mark in addition to the Notary.

Both witnesses should sign the document and the Notary's journal. One witness should legibly print the marker's name beside the mark on the document. It is recommended that a mark also be affixed in the Notary's journal.

Notarization Procedures. Because a properly witnessed mark is considered a signature under custom and law, no special Notary certificate is required. As required with any other signer, the marker must be positively identified.

Notarizing for Minors

Persons Under Age 18. Generally, individuals must reach the age of majority before they can handle their own legal affairs and sign documents for themselves. In New Jersey, the age of majority is 18. Normally, parents or court-appointed guardians will sign on a minor's behalf. In certain cases, where minors are engaged in business transactions or serving as witnesses in court, they may lawfully sign documents and have their signatures notarized.

Include Age Next to Signature. When notarizing for a minor, the Notary should ask the young signer to write his or her age next to the signature to alert any person relying on the document that the signer is a minor. The Notary is not required to verify the minor signer's age.

Identification. The method for identifying a minor is the same as that for an adult. However, determining the identity of a minor can be a problem, because minors often do not possess acceptable identification documents such as driver's licenses or passports. If the minor does not have an acceptable ID, then the other methods of identifying signers must be used, either the Notary's personal knowledge of the minor or the oath or affirmation of a personally known credible identifying witness who can identify the minor. (See "Credible Identifying Witnesses," pages 23–24.)

Authentication

Documents Sent Out of State. Documents notarized in New Jersey and sent to other states may be required by the entity receiving the document to bear written proof that the Notary's signature and seal (if used) are genuine and that the Notary had authority to act at the time of notarization. This process of proving the genuineness of an official signature and seal is called authentication or legalization.

In New Jersey, the proof is in the form of an authentication certificate attached to the notarized document by either the county clerk's office where the Notary's signature and certificate of official character are filed or the New Jersey State Treasurer's office.

The county clerk is restricted to providing authentication certificates only to Notaries residing — or working, in the case of nonresidents — in their counties, or to Notaries who have filed copies of their certificate of commission and qualification in their counties. The State Treasurer is authorized to issue authentication certificates relating to any Notary in the state, regardless of where the Notary has filed copies of the commission and qualification certificate (NJSA 52:7-15, 52:7-16).

Authentication certificates are known by different names: certificates of authority, certificates of capacity, certificates of authenticity, certificates of prothonotary, and "flags."

Procedure. It is not the Notary's responsibility to request an authentication certificate for a signer's notarized document. The individual seeking to obtain an authentication certificate must include a cover letter indicating the quantity of documents requiring authentication, along with the notarized documents, and the name, address, and telephone number of the person making the request. The request should be sent or presented to either the clerk of the county in which the Notary has filed the original or a copy of the certificate of commission and qualification or the State Treasurer's office.

For requests sent or presented to the state, the individual seeking an authentication may use the following information:

> Mailing address:
> State of New Jersey
> Department of the Treasury
> Division of Revenue and Enterprise Services
> Notary Public Section
> P.O. Box 452
> Trenton, NJ 08646
>
> Physical address (for in-person service):
> State of New Jersey
> Department of the Treasury
> Division of Revenue and Enterprise Services
> Notary Public Section
> 33 West State Street, 5th Fl.
> Trenton, NJ 08608-1214
>
> Telephone: (609) 292-9292

Fees. The State Treasurer charges $25 per document for service via mail ($5 for documents relating to an adoption). Expedited service is available for an additional $15 per document. Payment should be made by check or money order payable to the "Treasurer, State of New Jersey." If requesting authentication from a county, the individual should contact the county clerk for the fee in the particular county.

Documents Sent Out of Country. If the notarized document is going out of the United States, a chain authentication process may be necessary. Additional authentication certificates may have to be obtained from the U.S. Department of State in Washington, D.C., a foreign consulate in Washington, D.C. and a ministry of foreign affairs in the particular foreign nation.

Apostilles and the Hague Convention. More than 100 nations, including the United States, subscribe to a treaty under the auspices of the Hague Conference that simplifies authentication of notarized documents exchanged between any of these nations. The official name of this treaty, adopted by the Conference on October 5, 1961, is *The Hague Convention Abolishing the Requirement of Legalization for Foreign Public Documents.* (For a list of the subscribing countries, visit *www.hcch.net/index_en.php.*)

Under this Hague Convention, only one authentication certificate called an *apostille* is necessary to ensure acceptance in these subscribing countries. (*Apostille* is French for "notation".) It is not necessary to obtain an authentication certificate from the county prior to requesting an *apostille*.

In New Jersey, *apostilles* are issued by the State Treasurer's office (described above). *Apostilles* are not available from the county clerk.

An *apostille* must be specifically requested in writing, including the name, address, and telephone number of the person making the request. The letter also must identify the nation to which the document will be sent. The person requesting the *apostille* must send the letter, the notarized document, and the appropriate fee to the State Treasurer's office.

It should be noted that it is not the Notary's responsibility to obtain an *apostille*. It is the responsibility of the party sending the document out of the country.

Advertising

False or Misleading Advertising. A Notary's commission may be revoked or suspended if the Notary advertises or claims to have powers not authorized by law. For example, Notaries may not advertise that they have the authority to officially certify the translation of a document, since this is not a power given by New Jersey law.

Effective December 8, 2014, Notaries advertising their services, in either English or another language, must include the following notice in the advertisement: "I am not an attorney licensed to practice law and may not give legal advice about immigration or any other legal matter or accept fees for legal advice" (NJSA 52:7-11, 52:7-14, 52:7-17).

For practicing fraud or deceit in advertising or any other activity as a Notary, the Notary may be found guilty of a crime of the second degree or above (NJSA 57:7-20, 57:7-21).

Foreign Languages

Foreign-Language Documents. While New Jersey law does not directly address notarizing documents written in a language the Notary cannot read, it does set restrictions on the recording of documents written in a language other than English.

Any document conveying title to real property that is presented for recording in a county office must be completely in English, including the Notary certificate and any authentication certificates. (Proper names may be in a foreign language, as long as the letters used are those of the English language.) A non-English-language conveyance may only be recorded if accompanied by a duly certified English-language translation (NJSA 46:15-1.1).

As for notarizing other types of documents written in a language the Notary cannot read, while it is not expressly prohibited, there are difficulties and dangers in doing so.

The foremost danger is that the document may have been misrepresented to the Notary. Blatant fraud might remain undetected, the Notary's act might be misinterpreted in another country, and making a journal entry might be difficult.

Ideally, documents in foreign languages should be referred to New Jersey Notaries who read those languages. In large cities, such multilingual Notaries are often found in ethnic neighborhoods or in foreign consulates.

If a Notary chooses to notarize a document that he or she cannot read, then the Notary certificate should be in English or in a language the Notary can read, and the signature being notarized should be written in characters the Notary is familiar with.

Foreign-Speaking Signers. There should always be direct communication between the Notary and document signer — whether in English or any other language. The Notary should never rely on an intermediary or interpreter to determine a signer's willingness or awareness. A third party may have a motive for misrepresenting the circumstances to the Notary and/or to the signer.

Immigration

Do Not Give Advice. Nonattorney Notaries may never advise others on the subject of immigration, nor help others prepare immigration documents — and especially not for a fee. Notaries who offer immigration advice to others may be subject to penalties for the unauthorized practice of law.

Immigration Consultant. An immigration consultant renders non-legal services such as the completion of forms and applications, to determine or modify an individual's immigration or naturalization status under federal law.

An immigration consultant who is not licensed to practice law is guilty of a crime of the third degree if he or she uses or advertises any title, either in English or another language, which means or implies that the immigration consultant is licensed to practice law in New Jersey or any other jurisdiction of the United States (NJSA 2C:21-31).

Military-Personnel Notarizations

May Notarize Worldwide. Certain U.S. military personnel may notarize anywhere in the world for (U.S. Code, Title 10, Section 1044[a]):

- Members of any of the armed forces.

- Other persons eligible for legal assistance under U.S. Code Title 10, Section 1044, or under Department of Defense regulations.

- Persons serving with, employed by, or accompanying the armed forces outside the United States and its territories.

- Other persons subject to the Uniform Code of Military Justice outside the United States.

Under statutory authority, the following persons are authorized to act as Notaries (U.S. Code, Title 10, Section 1044[b]):

- Civilian attorneys serving as legal assistance attorneys

- Judge advocates, including reserve judge advocates when not in a duty status

- All adjutants, assistant adjutants, and personnel adjutants, including reserve members when not in a duty status

- All other members of the armed forces, including reserve members when not in a duty status, who are designated by regulations of the armed forces or by statute to have those powers

- For the performance of notarial acts outside the United States only, all employees of a military department or of the Coast Guard who are designated by regulations of the Secretary concerned or by statute to have those powers

Fee. Military-personnel Notaries may not charge or receive a fee for their services (U.S. Code, Title 10, Section 1044[c]).

Authentication. Authentication of a military-personnel notarization certificate is not required (U.S. Code, Title 10, Section 1044[d]).

Wills

Do Not Offer Advice. A Notary risks prosecution for the unauthorized practice of law in advising a signer how to proceed with a will. In addition, the Notary's ill-informed advice may adversely affect the affairs of the signer. The format of a will is dictated by strict laws of each state, and any deviation may result in nullification. In some cases, holographic (handwritten) wills have actually been voided by notarization.

A Notary should notarize a document described as a will only if a Notary certificate is provided or stipulated for each signer and the signers are not asking questions about how to proceed. Any such questions should be answered by an attorney.

Living Wills. Documents popularly called "living wills" may be notarized. These are not actual wills, but written statements of a signer's wishes concerning medical treatment in the event he or she is unable to issue instructions on his or her own behalf.

Self-Proved Wills. In New Jersey, self-proving wills may require the signatures of the testator and two witnesses to be notarized (NJSA 3B:3-5, 3B:3-7, 3B:3-8).

Certificate for Self-Proved Will. The Notary certificate for a self-proved will must be in substantially the following form (NJSA 3B:3-5):

State of New Jersey   )
) ss.
County of _____)

We, _____, the testator and the witnesses, respectively, whose names are signed to the attached or foregoing instrument, being duly sworn, do hereby declare to the undersigned authority that the testator signed and executed the instrument as his/her last will and that he/she had signed willingly (or willingly directed another to sign for him/her), and that he/she executed it as his/her free and voluntary act for the purposes therein expressed, and that each of the witnesses, in the presence and hearing of the testator, signed the will as witness and that to the best of his/her knowledge the testator was at that time 18 years of age or older, of sound mind and under no constraint or undue influence.

Testator _____
Witness _____
Witness _____

Subscribed, sworn to and acknowledged before me by _____, the testator, and subscribed and sworn to before me by _____ and _____, witnesses, this _____ day of _____ (month and year).

_____ (Signed) (Notary's Seal)
_____ (Official capacity of officer)

Advance Directives for Health Care

Purpose. Any individual may execute an advance directive for health care. The directive either must be signed and dated in the presence of two witnesses or must be acknowledged before a Notary Public (NJSA 26:2H-56).

If a Notary is asked to take the acknowledgment of the signer of an advance directive for health care, no special procedures are required. The Notary takes the signer's acknowledgment in the usual manner.

Electronic Notarization

Allowed But No Procedures Established. New Jersey has enacted the Uniform Electronic Transactions Act. This act states that, if the law requires that a signature or document be notarized, that requirement is met if the Notary's electronic signature and other required information (e.g., the Notary's name and commission expiration date) are attached to or logically associated with the notarized document (NJSA 12A:11-12).

At this time, however, New Jersey has not enacted laws or rules establishing the necessary procedures for electronic notarizations to take place.

Electronic Recording

The New Jersey State Division of Archives and Records Management has published administrative rules to govern the electronic recording of real property documents. The rules, adopted October 6, 2014, provide that an electronic document submitted for electronic recording in New Jersey must be notarized in compliance with the New Jersey Uniform Electronic Transactions Act. They also clarify that a county recorder has no duty to verify a Notary's electronic signature (NJ Administrative Code, Section 15:3-9.6).

MISCONDUCT, FINES AND PENALTIES

Misconduct

General Prohibitions. Although New Jersey statute sets out very little to define what may be construed as official misconduct, the online edition of the *New Jersey Notary Public Manual* defines some general acts that are prohibited.

A New Jersey Notary should never:

- Pre-date a certificate prior to the date of execution of the document.

- Share with another person a journal, seal, or other personalized Notary equipment.

- Prepare or draft legal documents or offer legal advice or advice on matters pertaining to land titles.

- Represent another person in a legal proceeding, especially in the capacity of a Notary.

- Collect delinquent bills or claims for others, especially in the capacity of a Notary.

NEW JERSEY NOTARY LAW PRIMER

Criminal Conviction. Conviction in New Jersey or any other state for a crime or any offense involving dishonesty — such as fraud or misrepresentation — or of a crime of the first or second degree may be reason for the State Treasurer to refuse to grant a Notary's commission (NJSA 52:7-20, 52:7-21).

Falsely Acting as a Notary. Any person who is not a Notary and who represents himself or herself as a Notary Public or any other public officer is guilty of a "disorderly persons offense" and may be ordered to pay a fine not to exceed $1000, to make restitution for monetary damages, or both (NJSA 2C:28-8, 2C:43-3).

Failure of Duty. Failure to fully and faithfully discharge the duties or responsibilities of a Notary — such as failing to complete a Notary certificate — may subject the Notary to charges of misconduct and removal from office.

Failure to Affix Name. On every Notary certificate, the Notary must affix, in addition to his or her official signature, his or her name by printing, typing, or stamping the name (NJSA 52:7-19).

Failure to include the required information may cause a document to be rejected and may subject a Notary to lawsuits by injured parties.

Overcharging. A Notary who charges more than the legally prescribed fees for executing a protest is subject to civil action in which the person overcharged may seek to recover $25 plus court costs (NJSA 22A:4-13).

Although the laws only prescribe penalties for protests, a Notary who charges more than the maximum statutory fee for any notarial act may be subject to charges of discrimination.

False Acknowledgment. A Notary must ensure that a certificate for an acknowledgment reflects the date the signer actually appeared before the Notary. A certificate that indicates a different date from that on which the signer actually appeared is considered to be fraudulent.

A Notary who knowingly completes a false certificate may be subject to criminal penalties.

Telephone Notarizations. New Jersey law expressly requires document signers to personally appear before the Notary at the time of notarization. Telephone notarizations are not permitted (NJSA 46:14-2.1).

Undue Influence. Since Notaries are appointed to serve as impartial witnesses, a Notary must never attempt to influence a person to execute or not to execute a document or transaction requiring a notarial act.

Misrepresentation. Anyone who knowingly creates or reinforces a false impression that he or she is licensed to practice law is guilty of a crime of the third degree. This includes using or advertising any title, either in English or another language, that means or implies that the person is licensed to practice law in New Jersey or any other jurisdiction of the United States (NJSA 2C:21-22).

Unauthorized Practice of Law. A nonattorney Notary is guilty of a crime of the fourth degree if he or she knowingly engages in the unauthorized practice of law. A nonattorney Notary is guilty of a crime of the third degree if he or she knowingly engages in the unauthorized practice of law and creates or reinforces a false impression that he or she is licensed to practice law, derives a benefit, or in fact injures another person (NJSA 2C:21-22).

Unauthorized Practice of Law as Immigration Consultant. A nonattorney immigration consultant is guilty of a crime of the third degree if he or she, either alone or together with a licensed attorney, engages in the practice of law. Further, any nonattorney immigration consultant is guilty of a crime in the third degree if he or she uses or advertises the title of lawyer, or equivalent terms, in English or any other language (NJSA 2C:21-31).

Right to Respond to Charges

Administrative Action Against Notary. Before the State Treasurer takes action against a commission, the accused Notary usually has a chance to respond to the charges. If there is no response from the accused Notary, the State Treasurer will take appropriate action. ■

New Jersey Laws Pertaining to Notaries Public

Reprinted on the following pages are pertinent sections of the New Jersey Statutes Annotated (NJSA) affecting Notaries and notarial acts. These statutes, along with this *Primer*, should be studied thoroughly before executing any notarial acts.

Citations at the end of each section indicate the most recent legislative action on the particular section. Three asterisks (***) in the text of a section indicate that irrelevant material has been omitted by the National Notary Association editors.

NOTE: Pursuant to the authority of the Executive Reorganization Act (NJSA 52:14C-1, et. seq.), all functions of the Division of Commercial Recording — which includes the Notary Public Section — have been transferred from the Secretary of State to the Department of the Treasury.

NEW JERSEY STATUTES ANNOTATED

Title 2A. Administration of Civil and Criminal Justice
Chapter 82. Documents, Records, and Other Written Instruments

2A:82-7. Certificate of protest as evidence.
The certificate of a notary public of this state or of any other state of the United States, under his hand and official seal accompanying any bill of exchange or promissory note which has been protested by such notary for nonacceptance or nonpayment, shall be received in all the courts of this state as competent evidence of the official character of such notary, and also of the facts therein certified as to the presentment and dishonor of

such bill or note and of the time and manner of giving or sending notice of dishonor to the parties to such bill or note.
L.1951 (1st SS), c.344.

2A:82-17. Certificates of acknowledgment or proof of instruments as evidence of execution thereof.

If any instrument heretofore made and executed or hereafter to be made and executed shall have been acknowledged, by any party who shall have executed it, or the execution thereof by such party shall have been proved by one or more of the subscribing witnesses to such instrument, in the manner and before one of the officers provided and required by law for the acknowledgment or proof of instruments in order to entitle them to be recorded, and, when a certificate of such acknowledgment or proof shall be written upon or under, or be annexed to such instrument and signed by such officer in the manner prescribed by law, such certificate of acknowledgment or proof shall be and constitute prima facie evidence of the due execution of such instrument by such party. Such instrument shall be received in evidence in any court or proceeding in this state in the same manner and to the same effect as though the execution of such instrument by such party had been proved by other evidence.
L.1951 (1st SS), c.344.

Title 2C. The New Jersey Code of Criminal Justice
Subtitle 2. Definitions of Specific Offenses
Part 4. Offenses Against Public Administration
Chapter 21. Forgery and Related Offenses

2C:21-22 Unauthorized practice of law; penalties.

1.a. A person is guilty of a crime of the fourth degree if the person knowingly engages in the unauthorized practice of law.

b. A person is guilty of a crime of the third degree if the person knowingly engages in the unauthorized practice of law and:

(1) Creates or reinforces, by any means, a false impression that the person is licensed to engage in the practice of law. As used in paragraph, "by any means" includes but is not limited to using or advertising the title of lawyer or attorney-at-law, or equivalent terms, in the English language or any other language, which mean or imply that the person is licensed as an attorney-at-law in the State of New Jersey or in any other jurisdiction of the United States; or

(2) Derives a benefit; or

(3) In fact causes injury to another.

c. For the purposes of this section, the phrase "in fact" indicates strict liability.

(cf: P.L.2011, c.209, s.1)

2C:21-31 Unauthorized practice of immigration law; penalties.

1. a. As used in this section:

(1) "Immigration consultant" means any person rendering services for a fee, including the completion of forms and applications, to another person in furtherance of that person's desire to determine or modify his status in an immigration or naturalization matter under federal law.

(2) "Immigration or naturalization matter" means any matter which involves any law, action, filing or proceeding related to a person's immigration or citizenship status in the United States.

(3) "Immigration-related document" means any birth certificate or marriage certificate; any document issued by the government of the United States, any foreign country, any state, or any other public entity relating to a person's immigration or naturalization status.

b. (1) Any immigration consultant not licensed as an attorney or counselor at law who engages in this State in the practice of law is guilty of a crime of the fourth degree.

(2) Any immigration consultant not licensed as an attorney or counselor at law who holds himself out to the public, either alone or together with, by or through another person, whether such other person is licensed as an attorney or counselor at law or not, as engaging in or entitled to engage in the practice of law, or as rendering legal service or advice, or as furnishing attorneys or counsel, in any immigration or naturalization matter is guilty of a crime of the third degree.

(3) Any immigration consultant not licensed as an attorney or counselor at law who assumes, uses or advertises the title of lawyer or attorney-at-law, or equivalent terms, in the English language or any other language which mean or imply that the immigration consultant is licensed as an attorney-at-law in the State of New Jersey or in any other jurisdiction of the United States, is guilty of a crime of the third degree.

c. Any person who knowingly retains possession of another person's immigration-related document for more than a reasonable time after the person who owns the document has submitted a written request for the document's return is guilty of a crime of the fourth degree.

d. Nothing in this section shall be construed to prohibit a person accredited as a representative by federal law pursuant to 8 CFR 292.2 from providing immigration services.

(cf: P.L.2011, c.209, s.3)

Chapter 28. Perjury and Falsification in Official Matters

2C:28-8. Impersonating a public servant or law enforcement officer.

a. Except as provided in subsection b. of this section, a person commits a disorderly persons offense if he falsely pretends to hold a position in the public service with purpose to induce another to submit to such pretended official authority or otherwise to act in reliance upon that pretense.

b. A person commits a crime of the fourth degree if he falsely pretends to hold a position as an officer or member or employee or agent of any organization or association of law enforcement officers with purpose to induce another to submit to such pretended official authority or otherwise to act in reliance upon that pretense.

L.1978, c.95; amended 2000, c.110.

Subtitle 3. Sentencing
Chapter 43. Authorized Disposition Of Offenders

2C:43-3. Fines and restitution.

A person who has been convicted of an offense may be sentenced to pay a fine, to make restitution, or both, such fine not to exceed: ...
***

c. $1,000.00, when the conviction is of a disorderly persons offense: ...
***

e. Any higher amount equal to double the pecuniary gain to the offender or loss to the victim caused by the conduct constituting the offense by the offender. In such case the court shall make a finding as to the amount of the gain or loss, and if the record does not contain sufficient evidence to support such a finding the court may conduct a hearing upon the issue. For purposes of this section the terms "gain" means the amount of money or the value of property derived by the offender and "loss" means the amount of value separated from the victim. The term "gain" shall also mean, where appropriate, the amount of any tax, fee, penalty, and interest avoided, evaded, or otherwise unpaid or improperly retained or disposed of; ...
***

The restitution ordered paid to the victim shall not exceed his loss, except that in any case involving the failure to pay any State tax, the amount of restitution to the State shall be the full amount of the tax avoided or evaded, including full civil penalties and interest as provided by law. In any case where the victim of the offense is any department or division of State government, the court shall order restitution to the victim. Any restitution imposed on a person shall be in addition to any fine which may be imposed pursuant to this section.

L.1978, c.95; amended 1979, c.178, s.83; 1981, c.290, s.37; 1987, c.76, s.34; 1987, c.106, s.10; 1991, c.329, s.2; 1995, c.20, s.6; 1995, c.417, s.2; 1997, c.181, s.12.

Title 12a. Commercial Transactions

12A:12-11. Notarized signatures or records.

11. If a law requires a signature or record to be notarized, acknowledged, verified, or made under oath, the requirement is satisfied if the electronic signature of the person authorized to perform those acts, together with all other information required to be included by other applicable law, is attached to or logically associated with the signature or record.

L.2001, c.116, s.11.

Title 17. Corporations And Institutions For Finance And Insurance
Subtitle 2. Financial Institutions
Part 3. Safe Deposit Companies
Chapter 14a. Safe Deposit Companies.

17:14A-51. Proceedings for unpaid rental.

If the amount due for the rental of any vault, safe deposit box or receptacle for the storage and safekeeping of personal property of any safe deposit company or bank, savings bank, or savings and loan association authorized to conduct a safe deposit business under the laws of this State has not been paid for one year, the safe deposit company, bank, savings bank, savings and loan association may at any time after the expiration of the year send a written notice by registered mail addressed to the lessee or lessees in whose name the vault, safe deposit or receptacle stands on its records, directed to the address on its records, that if the rental for the vault, safe deposit box or receptacle is not paid within 30 days after the date of the mailing of the notice, it will have the vault, safe deposit box or receptacle opened in the presence of one of its officers and of a notary public not in its employ, and the contents thereof, if any, placed in a sealed package by the notary public, marked by him with the name of the lessee or lessees in whose name the vault, safe deposit box or receptacle stands and the estimated value thereof, and the package so sealed and marked will be placed in one of the general vaults, safes or boxes of the safe deposit company, bank, savings bank or savings and loan association. The notary's proceedings shall be set forth in a certificate under his official seal, and the certificate shall be delivered to the savings and loan association, bank, savings bank or safe deposit company. The safe deposit company, bank, savings bank or savings and loan association shall have a lien on the contents of the vault, safe deposit box or receptacle so removed for the amount due to it for the rental of the vault, safe deposit box or receptacle up to the time of the removal of the contents, and for the costs and expenses, if any incurred in its opening, repairing and restoration for use. If the lien is not paid and discharged within one year from the opening of the vault, safe deposit box or receptacle and the removal of its contents, the safe deposit company, bank, savings bank or savings and loan association may sell the contents at public auction, or so much thereof as is required, to pay and discharge the lien and expenses of sale. A notice of the date, time and place of the sale shall be advertised in a newspaper having a general circulation in the county within which the principal office of the safe deposit company, bank, savings bank or savings and loan association is located, at least once a week for two successive weeks prior to the sale. The safe deposit company, bank, savings bank or savings and loan association may retain from the proceeds of sale the amount due to it for its lien and the expenses of sale. The balance of the proceeds of the sale and the unsold contents, if any, shall be held to be paid and delivered to the lessee or owner of the contents of the vault, safe deposit box or receptacle so sold.

If the balance of the proceeds of sale and the unsold contents, if any, remain unclaimed by the owner for the time prescribed in the "Uniform Unclaimed Property Act (1981)," R.S.46:30B-1 et seq., it shall be presumed to be abandoned and disposed of as therein provided.

L.1983, c.566, s.17:14A-51; amended 1989, c.58, s.4.

17:14A-52. Accessibility to vault, safe deposit box or receptacle.

The right of access to a vault, safe deposit box or receptacle rented to a lessee by a safe deposit company shall be governed by the rental agreement, the provisions of P.L.1955, c. 151 (C. 46:39-1 et seq.), R.S. 54:35-19 and R.S. 54:35-20.

L.1983, c. 566, s. 17:14A-52.

17:14A-53. Control of safe deposit company.

It shall be unlawful for any person or company, except with the approval of the commissioner, to acquire control of a safe deposit company incorporated under this chapter.

L.1983, c. 566, s. 17:14A-53.

Title 22a. Fees And Costs
Chapter 2. Civil Causes
Article 2. Superior Court, Law Division, and County Clerk's Office

22A:2-29. County clerk, deputy clerk of Superior Court, fees.

Upon the filing, indexing, entering or recording of the following documents or papers in the office of the county clerk or deputy clerk of the Superior Court, such parties, filing or having the same recorded or indexed in the county clerk's office or with the deputy clerk of the Superior Court in the various counties in this State in all civil or criminal causes, shall pay the following fees in lieu of the fees heretofore provided for the filing, recording or entering of such documents or papers:

***

Commissions and oaths--

Administering oaths to notaries public and, commissioners of deeds...$15.00

For issuing certificate of authority of notary to take proof, acknowledgment of affidavit $5.00

For issuing each certificate of the commission and qualification of notary public for filing with other county clerks.....................................$15.00

For filing each certificate of the commission and qualification of notary public in office of county clerk of county other than where such notary has qualified $15.00

***

L. 1953, c. 22, s.11; amended 1957, c. 224; 1965, c. 123, ss. 7,11; 1967, c. 113; 1980, c. 58, s. 2; 1985, c. 422, s. 4; 2001, c. 370, s. 2; 2002, c. 34, s. 31; 2004, c. 108, s. 3.

Chapter 4. Fees Of Certain State And County Officers

22A:4-14. Acknowledgments, proof, affidavits and oaths.

For a service specified in this section, commissioners of deeds, foreign commissioners of deeds, notaries public, judges and other officers authorized by law to perform such service, shall receive a fee as follows:

For administering an oath or taking an affidavit, ...$2.50
For taking proof of a deed,..$2.50
For taking all acknowledgments,..$2.50

For administering oaths, taking affidavits, taking proofs of a deed, and taking acknowledgments of the grantors in the transfer of real estate, regardless of the number of such services performed in a single transaction to transfer real estate,..$15.00

For administering oaths, taking affidavits and taking acknowledgments of the mortgagors in the financing of real estate, regardless of the number of such services performed in a single transaction to finance real estate, ...$25.00

L. 1953, c. 22, s. 11;amended 1964, c. 205; 2002, c. 34, s. 48.

Title 41. Oaths And Affidavits
Chapter 1. Forms, Solemnities, And Requisites Of Oaths And Affidavits

41:1-7. Seal not necessary to validity of oath or affidavit.

It shall not be necessary to the validity or sufficiency of any oath, affirmation or affidavit, made or taken before any of the persons named in section 41:2-1 of this title, that the same shall be certified under the official seal of the officer before whom made.

Chapter 2. Who May Administer Oaths and Affirmations
Article 1. Authority in General to Administer Oaths or Take Affidavits

41:2-1. Before whom (oaths, affirmations and affidavits) taken.

All oaths, affirmations and affidavits required to be made or taken by law of this State, or necessary or proper to be made, taken or used in any court of this State, or for any lawful purpose whatever, may be made and taken before any one of the following officers:

The Chief Justice of the Supreme Court or any of the justices or judges of courts of record of this State;

Masters of the Superior Court;

Municipal judges;

Mayors or aldermen of cities, towns or boroughs or commissioners of commission governed municipalities;

Surrogates, registers of deeds and mortgages, county clerks and their deputies;

Municipal clerks and clerks of boards of chosen freeholders;
Sheriffs of any county;
Members of boards of chosen freeholders;
Clerks of all courts;
Notaries public;
Commissioners of deeds;
Members of the State Legislature;
Attorneys-at-law and counsellors-at-law of this State.

This section shall not apply to official oaths required to be made or taken by any of the officers of this State, nor to oaths or affidavits required to be made and taken in open court.

Amended 1951, c. 302, s. 1; 1953, c. 39, s. 1; 1953, c. 428, s. 3; 1964, c. 165, s. 1; 1968, c. 169; 1970, c. 182; 1983, c. 495; 1986, c. 124; 2007, c. 73.

41:2-3. Oaths administered by notaries public in financial institution matters.

a. A notary public who is a stockholder, director, officer, employee or agent of a financial institution or other corporation may administer an oath to any other stockholder, director, officer, employee or agent of the corporation.

b. A notary public employed by a financial institution may follow directions or policies of the employer which provide that during the hours of the notary public's employment by the financial institution the notary public shall not administer oaths except in the course of the business of the employer.

As used in this section, "financial institution" means a State or federally chartered bank, savings bank, savings and loan association or credit union.

Amended 1997, c. 340.

Article 3. Oaths, Affirmations or Affidavits Out of State

41:2-17. Officers authorized to administer or take; jurat; certificate.

Any oath, affirmation or affidavit required or authorized to be taken in any suit or legal proceeding in this state, or for any lawful purpose whatever, except official oaths and depositions required to be taken upon notice, when taken out of this state, may be taken before any notary public of the state, territory, nation, kingdom or country in which the same shall be taken, or before any officer who may be authorized by the laws of this state to take the acknowledgment of deeds in such state, territory, nation, kingdom or country; and a recital that he is such notary or officer in the jurat or certificate of such oath, affirmation or affidavit, and his official designation annexed to his signature, and attested under his official seal, shall be sufficient proof that the person before whom the same is taken is such notary or officer. When, however, any other certificate is required by law to be annexed to the certificate of such officer, other than a notary public, for the recording of a deed acknowledged before him, a like certificate shall be annexed to his certificate of the taking of such oath.

Title 46. Property
Subtitle 3. Signatures, Seals, Acknowledgments and Proofs
Chapter 14. Acknowledgments and Proofs

46:14-2.1. Acknowledgment and proof.

a. To acknowledge a deed or other instrument the maker of the instrument shall appear before an officer specified in R.S. 46:14-6.1 and acknowledge that it was executed as the maker's own act. To acknowledge a deed or other instrument made on behalf of a corporation or other entity, the maker shall appear before an officer specified in R.S. 46:14-6.1 and state that the maker was authorized to execute the instrument on behalf of the entity and that the maker executed the instrument as the act of the entity.

b. To prove a deed or other instrument, a subscribing witness shall appear before an officer specified in R.S. 46:14-6.1 and swear that he or she witnessed the maker of the instrument execute the instrument as the maker's own act. To prove a deed or other instrument executed on behalf of a corporation or other entity, a subscribing witness shall appear before an officer specified in R.S. 46:14-6.1 and swear that the representative was authorized to execute the instrument on behalf of the entity, and that he or she witnessed the representative execute the instrument as the act of the entity.

c. The officer taking an acknowledgment or proof shall sign a certificate stating that acknowledgment or proof. The certificate shall also state:

(1) that the maker or the witness personally appeared before the officer;

(2) that the officer was satisfied that the person who made the acknowledgment or proof was the maker of or the witness to the instrument;

(3) the jurisdiction in which the acknowledgment or proof was taken;

(4) the officer's name and title;

(5) the date on which the acknowledgment was taken.

d. The seal of the officer taking the acknowledgment or proof need not be affixed to the certificate stating that acknowledgment or proof.

L. 1991, c. 308, s. 1.

46:14-4.1. Proof of instruments not acknowledged or proved.

If a deed or other instrument cannot be acknowledged or proved for any reason, the instrument may be proved in Superior Court by proof of handwriting or otherwise to the satisfaction of the court. Notice of the application in accordance with the Rules of Court shall be given to any party whose interests may be affected.

L. 1991, c. 308, s. 1.

46:14-4.2. Signatures.

For purposes of this title, a signature includes any mark made on a document by a person who thereby intends to give legal effect to the document. A signature also includes any mark made on a document on behalf of a person, with that person's authority and to effectuate that person's intent.

L. 1991, c. 308, s. 1.

46:14-6.1. Officers authorized to take acknowledgments.

a. The officers of this State authorized to take acknowledgments or proofs in this State, or in any other United States or foreign jurisdiction, are:

(1) an attorney-at-law;

(2) a notary public;

(3) a county clerk or deputy county clerk;

(4) a register of deeds and mortgages or a deputy register;

(5) a surrogate or deputy surrogate.

b. The officers authorized to take acknowledgments or proofs, in addition to those listed in subsection a., are:

(1) any officer of the United States, of a state, territory or district of the United States, or of a foreign nation authorized at the time and place of the acknowledgment or proof by the laws of that jurisdiction to take acknowledgments or proofs. If the certificate of acknowledgment or proof does not designate the officer as a justice, judge or notary, the certificate of acknowledgment or proof, or an affidavit appended to it, shall contain a statement of the officer's authority to take acknowledgments or proofs;

(2) a foreign commissioner of deeds for New Jersey within the jurisdiction of the commission;

(3) a foreign service or consular officer or other representative of the United States to any foreign nation, within the territory of that nation.

L. 1991, c. 308, s. 1.

Title 52. State Government, Departments and Officers
Subtitle 1. General Provisions
Chapter 7. Notaries Public

52:7-10. Short title.

This act shall be known and may be cited as the "Notaries Public Act of 1979."

L. 1979, c. 460, s 1.

52:7-11. Notaries public.

a. The State Treasurer shall appoint so many notaries public as the State Treasurer shall deem necessary to commission, who shall hold their respective offices for the term of five years, but may be removed from office at the pleasure of the State Treasurer.

b. A person desiring to be appointed and commissioned a notary public shall make application to the State Treasurer on a form prescribed by the

NEW JERSEY NOTARY LAW PRIMER

State Treasurer and endorsed by a member of the Legislature. Renewals thereof shall be made in the same manner as the original application.

The application form shall provide a notice to the applicant that a notary public who is not licensed as an attorney-at-law shall not use or advertise the title of lawyer or attorney-at-law, or equivalent terms, in the English language or any other language, which mean or imply that the notary public is licensed as an attorney-at-law in the State of New Jersey or in any other jurisdiction of the United States. The application form shall also state that a notary public who advertises his services in the English language or any other language is required to provide with such advertisement a notice which contains the following statement: "I am not an attorney licensed to practice law and may not give legal advice about immigration or any other legal matter or accept fees for legal advice."

c. The fee to be collected by the State Treasurer for that appointment or renewal shall be $25.00.

L.1979, c.460, s.2; amended 1987, c.435, s.21; 2014, c.48, s.3.

52:7-12. Minimum age.

No person shall be appointed a notary public unless he is 18 years of age or older.

L. 1979, c. 460, s. 3.

52:7-13. Appointment of nonresidents; requirements.

a. No person shall be denied appointment as a notary public on account of residence outside of this State, provided such person resides in a State adjoining this State and maintains, or is regularly employed in, an office in this State.

b. Before any such nonresident shall be appointed and commissioned as a notary public, he shall file with the State Treasurer an affidavit setting forth his residence and the address of his office or place of employment in this State.

c. Any such nonresident notary public shall file with the State Treasurer a certificate showing any change of residence or of his office or place of employment address in this State.

L.1979, c.460, s.4; amended 2014, c.48, s.4.

52:7-14. Oath; filing; certificate of commission and qualification.

a. Within three months of the receipt of his commission, each notary public shall take and subscribe an oath before the clerk of the county in which he resides, faithfully and honestly to discharge the duties of his office, and that he will make and keep a true record of all such matters as are required by law, which oath shall be filed with said clerk. The oath of office of a nonresident notary public shall be taken and subscribed before the clerk of the county in which he maintains his office or is employed in this State.

b. Upon the administration of said oath, the said clerk shall cause the notary public to indorse a certificate of commission and qualification and shall transmit said certificate to the State Treasurer within 10 days of the administration of said oath. After the administration of the oath, the clerk shall provide a notice to the person that a notary public who is not licensed as an attorney-at-law shall not use or advertise the title of lawyer or attorney-at-law, or equivalent terms, in the English language or any other language, which mean or imply that the notary public is licensed as an attorney-at-law in the State of New Jersey or in any other jurisdiction of the United States. The notice shall also state that a notary public who advertises his services, in the English language or any other language, is required to provide with such advertisement a notice which contains the following statement: "I am not an attorney licensed to practice law and may not give legal advice about immigration or any other legal matter or accept fees for legal advice."

c. The State Treasurer shall cancel and revoke the appointment of any notary public who fails to take and subscribe said oath within three months of the receipt of his commission and any appointment so canceled and revoked shall be null, void and of no effect.

L.1979, c.460, s.5; amended 2014, c.48, s.5.

52:7-15. State-wide authority; filing certificates of commission and qualification with county clerks.

a. A notary public who has been duly commissioned and qualified is authorized to perform his duties throughout the State.

b. Any notary public, after having been duly commissioned and qualified, shall, upon request, receive from the clerk of the county where he has qualified, as many certificates of his commission and qualification as he shall require for filing with other county clerks of this State, and upon receipt of such certificates the notary public may present the same, together with his autograph signature, to such county clerks as he may desire, for filing.

L. 1979, c. 460, s. 6.

52:7-16. County clerk to attach certificate of authority to notaries' certificates of proof, acknowledgments or affidavits.

The county clerk of the county in which a notary public resides or the county clerk of any county where such notary public shall have filed his autograph signature and certificate, as provided in section 6 of this act, shall, upon request, subjoin to any certificate of proof, acknowledgement or affidavit signed by the notary public, a certificate under the clerk's hand and seal stating that the notary public was at the time of taking such proof, acknowledgement or affidavit duly commissioned and sworn and residing in this State, and was as such an officer of this State duly authorized to take and certify said proof, acknowledgement or affidavit as well as to take and certify the proof or acknowledgement of deeds for the conveyance of lands, tenements or hereditaments and other instruments in writing to be recorded in this State; that said proof, acknowledgement or affidavit is duly executed and taken according to the laws of this State; that full faith and credit are and ought to be given to the official acts of the notary public, and that the county clerk is well acquainted with the handwriting of the notary public and believes the signature to the instrument to which the certificate is attached is his genuine signature.

L.1979, c. 460, s. 7

52:7-17. Fee; distribution of manual.

The State Treasurer shall, by regulation, fix a fee to be charged to each notary for the costs of printing and distribution to each applicant of a manual prescribing the powers, duties and responsibilities of a notary.

The manual shall specify that a notary public who is not licensed as an attorney-atlaw shall not use or advertise the title of lawyer or attorney-at-law, or equivalent terms, in the English language or any other language, which mean or imply that the notary public is licensed as an attorney or counselor at law in the State of New Jersey or in any other jurisdiction of the United States. The manual shall also state that a notary public who advertises his services in the English language or any other language is required to provide with such advertisement a notice which contains the following statement: "I am not an attorney licensed to practice law and may not give legal advice about immigration or any other legal matter or accept fees for legal advice." The manual shall also state that no person shall be appointed or reappointed a notary public if he has been convicted under the laws of this State of an offense involving dishonesty, including but not limited to a violation of section 1 of P.L.1997, c.1 (C.2C:21-31) or section 1 of P.L.1994, c.47 (C.2C:21-22), or a substantially similar crime under the laws of another state or the United States or of a crime of the second degree or above. The State Treasurer shall update the information contained in the manual and the Department of the Treasury's Internet website as appropriate.

L.1979, c.460, s.8; amended 2014, c.48, s.6.

52:7-18. Name change by notary, filing of statement.

After a notary public adopts a name different from that which he used at the time he was commissioned, and before he signs his name to any document which he is authorized or required to sign as notary public, he shall make and sign a statement in writing and under oath, on a form prescribed and furnished by the State Treasurer, setting out the circumstances under which he has adopted the new name. The statement shall set forth whether the new name has been adopted through marriage or by a change of name proceeding or otherwise, and such other information as the State Treasurer shall require.

The statement shall be filed in the office of the State Treasurer and in the office of the clerk of the county where he qualified as a notary public and in the office of the clerk of any county in which he may have filed a certificate of his commission and qualification.

Such statement, or a certified copy thereof, shall be evidence of the right of said notary public to continue to exercise the powers and privileges and perform the duties of a notary public in his changed and new name.

L.1979, c.460, s.9; amended 2014, c.48, s.7.

52:7-19. Affixation of name.

Each notary public, in addition to subscribing his autograph signature to any jurat upon the administration of any oath or the taking of any acknowledgement or proof, shall affix thereto his name in such a manner and by such means, including, but not limited to, printing, typing, or impressing by seal or mechanical stamp, as will enable the State Treasurer easily to read said name.

L.1979, c.460, s.10; amended 2014, c.48, s.8.

52:7-20. Offenses resulting in non-appointment, no reappointment of notary public.

No person shall be appointed or reappointed a notary public if he has been convicted under the laws of this State of an offense involving dishonesty, including but not limited to a violation of section 1 of P.L.1997, c.1 (C.2C:21-31) or section 1 of P.L.1994, c.47 (C.2C:21-22), or of a crime of the second degree or above, but nothing in this section shall be deemed to supersede P.L.1968, c. 282 (C.2A:168A-1 et seq.).

L.1981, c.487, s.1; amended 2011, c.209, s.5.

52:7-21. Conviction for certain offenses, crimes; denial of appointment.

No person shall be appointed a notary public if he has been convicted under the laws of another state, or of the United States, of an offense or crime involving dishonesty including but not limited to a violation of section 1 of P.L.1997, c.1 (C.2C:21-31) or section 1 of P.L.1994, c.47 (C.2C:21-22), or a crime of the second degree or above, but nothing in this section shall be deemed to supersede.

L.1981, c.487, s.2; amended 2014, c.48, s.9.

NEW JERSEY RULES OF CIVIL PROCEDURE

Rule 4:12. Persons before whom depositions may be taken; authority

4:12-1. Within the state

Within the State, depositions shall be taken before a person authorized by the laws of this State to administer oaths.

4:12-2. Without the state but within the United States

Outside this State but within the United States or within a territory or insular possession subject to the dominion of the United States, depositions may be taken before a person authorized to administer oaths by the laws of this State, of the United States or of the place where the examination is held.

4:12-3. In foreign countries

In a foreign country depositions shall be taken (a) on notice before a secretary of embassy or legation, consul general, consul, vice consul, or consular agent of the United States, or (b) before such person or officer as may be appointed by commission or under letters rogatory. A commission or letters rogatory shall be issued only when necessary or convenient, on application and notice, and on such terms and with such directions as are appropriate. Officers may be designated in notices or commissions either by name or descriptive title and letters rogatory may be addresses. "To the Appropriate Judicial Authority in (here name the country)."

4:12-4. Disqualification for interest

No deposition shall be taken before or by a person who is a relative, employee or attorney of a party or relative or employee of such attorney or is financially interested in an action.

NEW JERSEY RULES OF CRIMINAL PROCEDURE

Rule 3:13. Depositions; Discovery

3:13-2. Depositions

(a) When and how taken. If it appears to the judge of the court in which the indictment or accusation is pending that a material witness may be unable to attend or may be prevented from attending the trial of the indictment or accusation, or any hearing in connection therewith, the court, prevent injustice, may upon motion and notice to the parties order that the testimony of such witnesses be taken, orally by deposition as provided in civil actions and that any designated books, papers, documents or tangible objects, not privileged, be produced at the same time and place. If a witness is committed for failure to give bail to appear to testify at a trial or hearing, the court on written motion of the witness and upon notice to the parties may direct that his deposition be taken, and after the deposition has been subscribed the court may discharge the witness. The transcript of all depositions shall be filed with the county clerk as provided in civil actions.

(b) Use. [Omitted.]

(c) Objections to admissibility. Objections to receiving a deposition or part thereof in evidence may be made as provided in civil actions.

NEW JERSEY ADMINISTRATIVE CODE

Title 15. State
Chapter 3. Records Retention
Subchapter 9. Rules Regarding Electronically Submitted Documents Affecting Real Property in the Offices of New Jersey County Clerks and Registers of Deeds and Mortgages

15:3-9.6 Notarization of documents

An electronic document shall be notarized under provisions contained in the New Jersey Uniform Electronic Transactions Act, N.J.S.A. 12A:12-11, Notarized signatures or records. County recorders have no responsibility for verifying or authenticating notary signatures. ■

About the NNA

Since 1957, the National Notary Association — a nonprofit educational organization — has served the nation's Notaries Public with a wide variety of instructional programs and services.

As the country's clearinghouse for information on Notary laws, customs and practices, the NNA educates Notaries through publications, seminars, webinars, online training, annual conferences, its website and the NNA® Hotline that offers immediate answers to specific questions about notarization.

The Association is perhaps most widely known as the preeminent source of information for and about Notaries. NNA works include the following:

- *The National Notary*, a magazine for NNA members featuring how-to articles and practical tips on notarizing

- *Notary Bulletin*, an online newsletter that keeps NNA members and customers up to date on developments affecting Notaries, especially new state laws and regulations

- *Sorry, No Can Do!* series, four volumes that help Notaries explain to customers and bosses why some requests for notarizations are improper and cannot be accommodated

- *U.S. Notary Reference Manual*, an invaluable resource for any person relying upon the authenticity and correctness of legal documents

- *Notary Public Practices & Glossary*, a definitive reference book on Notary procedures and widely hailed as the Notary's bible

- State *Notary Law Primers*, short guidebooks that explain a state's Notary statutes in easy-to-understand language

- *The Notary Public Code of Professional Responsibility*, a comprehensive and detailed code of ethical and professional conduct for Notaries

- *The Model Notary Act*, prototype legislation conceived in 1973 and updated in 1984, 2002 and 2010 by an NNA-recruited panel of secretaries of state, legislators and attorneys, and regularly used by state legislatures in revising their Notary laws

- *Notary Signing Agent Training Course*, a manual covering every aspect of signing agent procedures that prepares candidates for the Notary Signing Agent Certification Examination developed by the NNA

- Public-service pamphlets informing the general public about the function of a Notary, including *What Is A Notary Public?* printed in English and Spanish

In addition, the NNA offers the highest quality professional supplies, including official seals and stamps, embossers, recordkeeping journals, jurat stamps, thumbprinting devices and Notary certificates.

Though dedicated primarily to educating and assisting Notaries, the NNA supports implementing effective Notary laws and informing the public about the Notary's vital role in modern society. ■

Index

A
Acknowledgments......................9–11
Address change 7
Advance directives for health
  care...46
Advertising....................................42–44
Affidavits 11–12
Affirmations 15–17
Apostille......................................42
Application...................................2–4
Authentication...........................40–43
Authorized acts............................8–9
Awareness.......................................22

B
Beneficial interest...........................36
Blank spaces...................................36
Bond...4–5

C
Certificate, Notary.....................29–32
Certified copies............................... 9
Copy certification by document
  custodian.. 9
Credible identifying witness 23–24
Criminal conviction 48

D
Death of Notary............................... 7
Delaware Notary, qualification....... 3
Depositions...............................12–13
Disqualifying interest................36–37

E
Electronic notarization 46–47
Electronic recording.......................47
Employer/Notary agreement....37–38
Errors and omissions insurance...4–5

F
Failure of duty 48
Failure to affix name 48
False certificate 32, 48
Falsely acting as Notary 48
Faxes 35
Fees 34–35
Financial interest............................36
Foreign languages 43

H
*Hague Convention Abolishing the
  Requirement of Legalization for
  Foreign Documents* 42

I
Identification..............................22–26
Identification documents..........24–25
Immigration 44, 49
Impartiality.....................................36
Incomplete documents..................36

J
Journal of notarial acts..............26–29
Jurats 13–15
Jurisdiction....................................... 6

67

L

Liability 4
Loose certificates 31
L.S. (*locus sigilli*) 33

M

Marriages 9
Military-personnel
   notarizations 44–45
Minors 39–40
Misconduct 47–49

N

Name change 7–8
New York Notary, qualification 3

O

Oath of office 5–6
Oaths 15–17
Overcharging 35, 48

P

Penalties 47–49
Pennsylvania Notary, qualification . 3
Personal appearance 22
Personal knowledge of identity 23
Photocopies 35
Proof of execution by subscribing
   witness 17–19
Protests 19–21

R

Reasonable care 38
Refusal of service 37
Relatives 36–37
Resignation 6

S

Seal, Notary 32–34
Signature by mark 39
Signature, Notary 30
SS, SCT (*scilicet*) 29–30
Statement of particulars 30

T

Telephone notarizations 48–49
Term of office 6
Testimonium clause 30

U

Unauthorized acts 9
Unauthorized practice of
   law 38–39, 49
Undue influence 49

V

Venue 29–30

W

Willingness 22
Wills 45–46
Witnessing safe deposit box
   opening 21